"*The Deep Down Things* is no regular, feel-good story. It is a modern epiphany of forest sounds and mud-caked hearts, gripping and transcendent. Amber and Seth Haines, at their shimmering best, nurture hope (and humor) from our darkest nights. Held in the sweet spot where honesty and faithfulness collide, this book will rattle your bones. It will shake your secrets loose. It will lead you to the feast."

—**Shannan Martin**, author of *Start with Hello*
and *The Ministry of Ordinary Places*

"Every time I sat down to read this book, it felt like my body was taking a deep breath. To be guided with such authenticity, to be led by two modern Ozark mystics who have been in the tall grass of despair and grief, to be seen in such a deep-down way . . . you will not regret one moment spent inside this work of thoughtful love and spine-straightening hope."

—**Erin Moon**, resident Bible scholar
on *The Bible Binge* podcast

"Honest to the bone, Seth and Amber dig deep to name the pain that has marred their stories, yet they artfully share that even in the darkest of seasons, hope blossoms and healing is our divine right no matter what we've lost or when we lost our way."

—**Tiffany Bluhm**, author of *Prey Tell:
Why We Silence Women Who Tell the Truth
and How Everyone Can Speak Up*

"Amber and Seth Haines challenge the narrative of despair that hangs in the air all around us, not by dismissing the darkness but by staring defiantly back with the love-light of hope in their eyes. In these pages, the faith, forgiveness, and healing the Haineses share are hard-won and costly. By offering their story, this book will remind you of an even deeper story: the foundations of the universe rest not in the chaos of despair but in the nail-pierced hands of love."

—**Haley Stewart**, author of *The Grace of Enough*;
editor of Word on Fire Spark

"In this book, Amber and Seth have written one sacred invitation after another—invitations into deeper honesty and deeper faith, more beauty and more grit, bolder raging and bolder praying. This book is beautifully written and heavily sense-drenched—if you love gardens and music and fishing and old homes and stories and families and land and silence, you'll treasure these pages. And if your heart has been broken, you'll find a kind companion in these pages too—as I read, I began to feel both more human and more beloved. I want to press this book into the hands of every person I know who is suffering and also seeking something sacred, which is basically all of us."

—**Shauna Niequist**, *New York Times* bestselling author
of *I Guess I Haven't Learned That Yet*

"Amber and Seth Haines give us a powerful testament to the human spirit and the power of the Spirit we can tap to overcome adversity and despair. With honesty and vulnerability, they share their personal struggles and the discovery they found as they leaned into pain, sickness, and disappointments. As Amber so eloquently states, 'This book is a light along the way' for those feeling a little lost or unseen. The practical advice and inspiring stories will offer hope and motivation to all who read them. This book will draw you closer to your own strength in God and leave you feeling empowered to face whatever challenges life throws your way."

—**Latasha Morrison**, author of the *New York Times*
bestseller *Be the Bridge: Pursuing God's Heart
for Racial Reconciliation*

"This book, a memoir laced in pain, is a mirror and a balm and an invitation to think truly and critically and kindly on your own story and your own faith."

—**Annie F. Downs**, *New York Times* bestselling
author of *That Sounds Fun*

"In *The Deep Down Things*, Seth and Amber Haines, with their stunning writing, light a torch and guide you into the deeper streams. The vulnerability, accessibility, and invitation to try on what they write about in each chapter makes this more than a book; it is rather a holy experience. What you hold in your hands is special and timely, and if embodied, it can do wonders within."

—**Steve Carter**, pastor and author
of *The Thing Beneath the Thing*

THE
DEEP
DOWN
THINGS

THE
DEEP
DOWN
THINGS

Practices for Growing Hope in Times of Despair

AMBER C. HAINES AND SETH HAINES

BrazosPress

a division of Baker Publishing Group
Grand Rapids, Michigan

Published by Brazos Press
a division of Baker Publishing Group
Grand Rapids, Michigan
www.brazospress.com

Printed in the United States of America

Library of Congress Cataloging-in-Publication Data
Names: Haines, Mary Amber, 1979– author. | Haines, Seth, author.
Title: The deep down things : practices for growing hope in times of despair / Amber C. Haines and Seth Haines.
Description: Grand Rapids, Michigan : Brazos Press, a division of Baker Publishing Group, [2023] | Includes bibliographical references.
Identifiers: LCCN 2023014160 | ISBN 9781587435638 (paperback) | ISBN 9781587436161 (casebound) | ISBN 9781493438501 (ebook) | ISBN 9781493438518 (pdf)
Subjects: LCSH: Hope—Religious aspects—Christianity. | Despair—Religious aspects—Christianity.
Classification: LCC BV4638 .H25 2023 | DDC 234/.25—dc23/eng/20230601
LC record available at https://lccn.loc.gov/2023014160

Baker Publishing Group publications use paper produced from sustainable forestry practices and post-consumer waste whenever possible.

23 24 25 26 27 28 29   7 6 5 4 3 2 1

To Joseph and Lindsey Mason

CONTENTS

A LETTER TO THE READER

Dear Reader,

There are a few things I want you to know before you dive in with us here.

Most of the time spent writing creative nonfiction isn't in the writing at all. It's in living the story, and the season of living this story lasted way longer than I expected. We moved into a new home soon after things in our world fell apart—more on that later—and then immediately, COVID-19 changed the whole world. We went from being a family with a house full of people each week to being a family who couldn't remember the last time a friend had knocked on our door. Like so many others—maybe like you—all we had were ourselves.

When the pandemic first hit, I secretly enjoyed the pause in our insane schedules, my kids being safe and at home, all the bread Seth was baking, and how much attention I was able to give my garden. Up until I got COVID, that season was one of healing for me in some ways, because there wasn't much else to do but heal. We took long family walks. The boys made up games, and I kept the house straight. After a little while, the house started shrinking, though, and the piles covering the dusty desk in the corner of our tiny bedroom mocked me.

1

In that season, I told myself I couldn't write because my house was full of hungry people who needed help with virtual school. To really heal from the experiences of the years before COVID, though, I needed to write because that's how I work. Writing brings me healing, but I don't think I was ready to know what would fall onto the page if I really committed to the work. I kept saying that I was afraid some primal animal sounds would peal from my body if I ever started to give voice to what was going on inside me. Like many others, I was stuck in survival mode and sharing small spaces with too many people, which, come to find out, is a wet blanket to the passionate little fires I usually keep burning. So, I just kept not writing.

When church doors finally opened up, we had somewhere to go, even though it wasn't back to our old church, but other than that, the garden was my paradise. Even in winter, I had put little hoops over what I'd planted and kept kale and carrots growing longer than ever before. I watched some amazing cold-hardy flowers press through the coldest winter of my life. I lifted the covering over the hoops like a veil. There was always a thing to notice or a plant growing that should have been long dead.

When I got COVID, I spent fourteen days alone in my bedroom. I didn't read a word, and I tried to watch only one movie. I sat up in bed all fourteen days like a dull zombie with my brain shut down, and it would be well over a year before I felt like it started to come back. I asked for an MRI because I thought it was possible my brain had shrunk down to the size of a chicken nugget, and I spent a long time thinking, *This is just the way things are now*. I believed I would never come close to writing another book, which is why I asked Seth to write half of this one with me. I had no clue how we would pull it off, but I knew he'd be by my side whether we did or not. We critique each other well, and we're usually a creative match. I'm glad my lack of faith brought us together like this.

Seth also has a thing or two to say about despair. He's had his own, but he's also played the role of holding out hope for me, of believing in me and for me when I didn't have a hair of faith left. He believed when I thought I would never read or write again. I had to relearn how to do them, and along the way, I continued to say, "I can't." But all he ever said to me in return was "I know you can," and without knowing how, I slowly began to believe him. What is it like to watch someone you love stop believing? To believe for you both? Ask Seth.

It's been a journey, and though the subtitle of this book is *Practices for Growing Hope in Times of Despair*, we do not claim to offer you a formula for getting out of depression, much less despair. If you are in despair, we hope you'll do some of the things we write about in this book because we believe they are healthy human practices, but also, please pick up the phone and make an appointment. Take the medicine you need to take. Talk to professionals. Reach out to someone. Take yourself and your pain seriously.

Let me say it even more clearly: This is not a how-to book. Rather, this is a light along the way. A thing to hold in your hands if you ever feel out-of-body. We've written this book to share where we have found hope. We do not believe that hope is some ethereal thing floating out there in the great beyond. Hope is a thing that is here and now, and it requires some participation. Like love, hope has a way of acting. So we decided to write a book together about some of the ways we've practiced interacting with hope. Maybe a story here will encourage you more than participating in any of the practices. I don't know.

As for our pedigree, our authority, just remember as you read that I am a seminary dropout. I follow Jesus, but I am not a theologian. I love science, but I am not a scientist. I love to grow things, but I am not a farmer—yet. See what I'm trying to say? I have a degree in creative writing and half of a master's of fine arts in poetry. So that's what this is: our attempt to create a little art that shows something of hope. Maybe it'll offer you some presence, an idea or two, or just a little validation that you might have a few more marbles than I do. We are here to bring solidarity, and we aim to do it with truth and beauty and maybe a little dark humor. This is our journey, and it will look and sound very different from yours.

Two final words: First, what follows is an account of hard things that happened to us over the past several years—both as we remember them and as they are documented—and how they affected us. Second, we have landed in a very Catholic place, which is to say that we entered the Roman Catholic Church during the pandemic. That's a whole story to itself, but while we're on the topic, please know that this book is not a piece of Catholic propaganda. We don't write expecting you—or any readers, for that matter—to land in the same place we did. That is another way to say, this book is not an apologetic for anything other than hope. What do I hope of you? First, I hope you'll give us a little grace if we get a little too Catholic for your taste and that you'll look to the deep truth under our religious practice. I also hope you'll keep us honest. I expect you'll have to scoff once in a while. If I ever get the chance, I might playfully scoff at you, and I hope we can share a laugh about that. More than anything, though, I hope we'll tend to believe each other and the stories we have to tell. We're telling ours as best we can and hope to be just offensive enough, just hopeful enough, just idealistic enough, just *whatever* enough.

Let our journey be ours. We're glad you're here, glad to see you taking yours.

I trust you're doing that.

Amber

one

KNOW THE HOPE OF SAINTS

Seth: Eat the Flowers

In the beginning, there was dust. And the dust strained and stretched across the great swath of the central Texan plains dappled and dotted with scrub brush, mesquite trees, and white sheets flagging on the clothesline. In the silver morning, the mist rose from the grass, greeted the fathers on their way to the freight docks and factories, comforted the mothers and their dreams of equal work and equal pay, cocooned the children as they devoured bowl after bowl of Cheerios on the back porch. In the beginning, the mist rose against my own naked knees, my five-year-old cheeks, my closed eyelids, my ravenous hunger. These are my first memories of the beginning.

In the beginning, there were songs of bobwhites and long-tailed birds and the occasional coyote. There were songs of people too, songs of choirs with words so thick they covered church walls and living rooms like honey. In one of those living rooms, a large man played the keyboard. He sang some song about Jesus while a new puppy—Todd—sat at his feet.

I inherited that puppy for a short season, and he made his own songs when the Texas moon broke the horizon. Those songs—the birds', coyotes', choirs', Todd's—still cover my memory. Those songs are still good.

Dust and slivers of sun cutting through the morning, songs of creatures and choirs and the very earth herself rising—these were high art, the art of a universe that hummed and vibrated in the air around me. The preacher named that humming "God" and said this God had spoken all the world into existence. Everything, then, was the echo of divine speech.

In the beginning, there was a song, and the song was God's, and the song came and dwelt among us, filling up the whole world. It wasn't a surface song. It vibrated beneath what's seen, way down, in the "deep down things," as Gerard Manley Hopkins wrote.[1] This song was as real as my heartbeat, the rhythmic cicada songs, the pulse of the ocean. It was from God, and it was in me and the world around me.

I was too young and too Texan, so I didn't know Hopkins's work, but I think I shared some of his boyhood nature. I've since learned that 150 years ago, in Victorian England, the English poet came into his own images and impressions. He—a boy who was destined to be one of the world's master poets—was so convinced in the deep down things that he took his brothers into the forest and made them eat the flowers so they could understand more than the appearance of a thing. When I first read this, I wondered whether he might be insane, but now I understand: the sacramental energy of God filled everything in the world around him. Creation was neither abstract nor outside of humanity. It was a thing meant to be taken in, ingested, fully experienced. This was what it meant to commune with God.

Hopkins knew that God spoke beauty and flame into the earth's first day of existence, and then that same God inhabited that earth, taking the form of his creation—man.

And when that inhabiting God—Christ—broke the sting of death and the bonds of gravity, he left all of us more than access to heaven. He left us tangible pieces of himself for the taking, pieces that allow us to experience Christ, who'd been not just on earth but in the earth, every little piece of it. This was the gospel according to Gerard Manley Hopkins.

Born into an upper-middle-class Anglican family, Hopkins could have taken a predictable path—a successful business, the Sunday service, plum pudding on Christmas. He could have stretched socked feet by the fire well into his later decades, could have spent the evening hours scratching a hunting hound behind the ears, content to have risen above the station of a factory worker eking out an unfair wage in deplorable conditions. Contentment with English comforts wasn't in his bones, though. Poetry was. Sacrament was. Christ was. As Dana Gioia puts it, a "brave new world filled his senses with the sacramental energy of creation where every bird, tree, branch, and blossom trembled with divine immanence."[2]

In his early twenties, convinced that the sacramental energy was present and potent in the bread and wine of the Eucharist, Hopkins left his nominal Anglican life and broke the bonds with his family faith, with the only world he knew. He joined the Catholic Church, burned every scrap of poetry he'd written, and left the easy hopes of middle-class comfort behind. He joined the priesthood—the Jesuits no less—and I wonder: How did it feel to come into a religious home while being cast out of a family home?

For seven years, the man who had poetry in his bones went without writing a single poem. When he finally returned to the page, it was with an experimental flourish. Did he know those experiments wouldn't be appreciated in his lifetime? Did he know that even as he attempted to convey the

sacramental energy through the images and impressions of
his poetry, readers wouldn't quite get it? I'm not sure that I
get it, at least not all the way, but these words from "God's
Grandeur" express so much of what I've felt over these last
few years:

> And for all this, nature is never spent;
>> There lives the dearest freshness deep down
>>> things;
> And though the last lights off the black West went
>> Oh, morning, at the brown brink eastward,
>>> springs—
> Because the Holy Ghost over the bent
>> World broods with warm breast and with ah!
>>> bright wings.[3]

The presence of God in preternatural things unseen by
most of us filled him up. And it was those things that pulled
him through life. Not the middle-class comforts of former
Oxford classmates. Not the success of a poet either, because
he died having published very little. His calling—to trans-
pose the energy of God onto the page—was the ultimate
deep down thing, and he did it despite the ambivalence of
family, friends, and potential publishers. He did it despite
the despair of what must have felt like a lackluster vocation,
at least in his lifetime.

I wonder how Hopkins would feel about the summation
of his legacy written by Margaret R. Ellsberg in *The Gospel
in Gerard Manley Hopkins*: "Decades after his death, Hopkins became suddenly and then increasingly recognized for a
poetic product which not only influenced countless writers
who came after, but also articulated a religious vocation
that served the greater glory of God through art."[4] I wonder
whether he was surprised when his star rose well after his
death. Did he look down from heaven when he was recog-

nized as a postmortem poet extraordinaire and say, "Yeah . . . that just about figures"?

I think about his poetry a lot, and not just because of the work itself. I think about it because, as far as I can recall, he was the first poet Amber introduced me to. When she studied poetry at the University of Arkansas, she was drawn to his work as a traveling companion of sorts. It was Hopkins who saw the flame of God in a leaf or a blade of grass or those great kingfishers that, as Hopkins wrote, "catch fire."[5] It was Hopkins who used language as an experiment in speaking God. Those images, those experiments showed Amber just how poetry or any other art can translate the sacramental energy of God in the world. And ever since, she's tried to use her words to do the same, whether in poetry, in sermons, or in the kinds of online spaces Hopkins would never have imagined.

It's been a while since those university years. Life has done what it's done, and like most, we've lost a good bit to the refining fires of life. Amber was a curate in an Anglican church, and I was the worship leader there. She was on the path to ordination, but the way grew dark, unnavigable. Once, she closed her eyes as the church prayed over her, and the only vision that came was that of being beaten by a shepherd. It'd take her months to decipher that riddle, but when she did, a pit opened underneath her.

That's when she began losing sleep, hair, identity. Muscle twitches set in. A doctor stuck needles in her thighs and ran electricity through them to test her for ALS. But it wasn't ALS. It was the endless firing of stressed-out nerves. Everything was cracking, so Amber shared the truth behind the stress with our friends: continuing in ministry required finding a healthier situation, one in which the world did not center around the size of a man's fragile ego. So, we put money down on a rental house in Atlanta and planned to move to a church where she might participate in or simply witness healthy ministry. But our friends countered, asked us to stay because things could be better. There could be more accountability, more participation, a better working environment. They said the church would struggle if we moved, which is a heavy thing to strap on someone's shoulders. We agreed because Fayetteville was *our* hometown—not the hometown of the priest who was over her curacy—and if our friends were in, we'd try to make it work.

These promises were too hard to keep. Things didn't change. They grew worse. The working relationship between Amber and the priest grew more unhealthy. Less stable. More jealous or territorial or manipulative or whatever. And it all culminated in this: Amber turned in her cassock and set fire to the hope that she would, one day, be an *ordained* minister of the gospel.

For months, Amber fell headfirst into an endless darkness, and all I could do was watch. There was no changing the circumstances, no fixing things. But in the waiting, that song of sacramental energy came, the song Hopkins knew well. She suggested we visit our local Catholic parish—a church I was already attending with some regularity—and on our first day there, the priest asked the men to stand and own the fact that they had a good bit of spiritual work to do. He called us to account. Though the moment spoke to me, it didn't impact me the same way it did Amber. Men taking responsibility, confessing, repenting. Then everyone filed to the front for their healing, for the body and blood of the Eucharist. It somehow recollected her broken pieces.

After that service, Amber ached for the Eucharist. She said it was the only thing that made sense to her anymore. "Either it's true or nothing is," she said after only a few visits, and that was that.

She had withdrawn from her seminary classes, and after a time, she enrolled instead in classes to better understand the Catholic Church, classes known as the Rite of Christian Initiation of Adults. Less than a year later, she and I recited the same liturgies that had filled Hopkins's mouth. We participated in the same confession, said the same act of contrition. We made our way to the church, consumed the same body and blood Hopkins had.

Along the way, Amber came to believe that Christ sang into the world through all the acts of the church. He was found in the bread and wine, in all the other sacraments too. But his song was also found outside the walls of any structure, in the sacramental energy of earthly things—flowers, birds, friends, feasts, bread, wine, prayers, art, the land, the words of the saints. All these things began pulling her from despair because that's what happens when we look for Christ's presence in the world all around us.

There are days when I wish I could sit with Hopkins as a spiritual director or even just an acquaintance who drinks coffee at Hail Fellow Well Met. (Yes, we name our coffee shops after obscure English phrases now.) There are things I wish I could ask him, like: What did you do with the pain that the sacramental energy soothes but can't erase? When your work was unappreciated? When you were discounted, discredited, or dismissed? What should I do when I feel discarded like a heel of bread? What should any of us do when pandemics rage or marriages fail or loved ones die or church leaders make too much of their own egos or the best laid plans of men bite the dust? Whenever whatever threatens to undo us and our God-given work, where can we find relief? I suspect he'd say to look around and notice all the places where God shows his divine love. Then spend time in those places.

In his darkest days, Hopkins found God hidden in the things of earth. He found him in the trout, the flowers, the

11

sea, the bread, the wine, the poems he wrote. And he showed us in that way of finding God, there was something like hope.

Amber: The Gothic Middle

Even though it's the pitch of night, this is not a dark place.

Peering inside through the sliding glass door, I can see Seth behind the kitchen counter with our four boys lined up at the bar. All the lights are on, and I can tell it's maniacally loud in there, so I've decided to sit outside for another minute alone with these mysterious yard boulders that encircle the fire pit. We don't really know how they got here at the back of this garden, but it must have taken some effort. We only know they were made as a place to gather people up, reminiscent of a mini Stonehenge, some gateway to a grand story, a little wrinkle in time.

The kids love to climb and jump from one boulder to the next. They contain flecks of pink, green, and gray granite and give our yard an ancient depth. We tend to gather in a circle as a family with our best friends here, where we imagine people have gathered for ages. I also tend to sit alone here just to gather myself.

I face the raised beds at night just like I do in the day. Fireflies blink deep into the bamboo stand beyond the rocks. In the summer, the mosquitoes have me like charcuterie, but I don't pay attention. I pay closer attention to what's gathering within me, what comes to view in the dark, the things I see clearly here, and all the things I recognize that I can't unsee no matter how hard I close my eyes.

Here in the garden, especially in the dark, I often think of my confirmation saint, Mary Magdalene, because she's a pillar among us. She herself has been a longtime gathering place for brokenhearted women who found their comfort in the only place it could be found. Mary is my garden friend because she had her own garden experiences that sent her on toward the path of her vocation.

I do wonder if she went back to visit the garden once she found her path. Right now, I'm compelled at all hours of the day to visit my own raised beds and swaying blooms. Even when no work is required, the garden brings order to my body and mind. It's also given me something to tend to in place of what I've given up—my beloved work as a curate and ordinand, my sense of place in a church community that was my life. This circle of boulders has backdropped my frantic sorting through the loss of my identity and vocational ministry, the use of my voice, and the trust developed in long-haul friendships. I have sat for hours here, blank-minded, a slate wiped clean of emotion, even of despair. I have also cried so loudly here that my neighbors heard. I have journaled pages and pages and burned them in the middle of these rocks. I have tried to make sense. I have begged God. I have heard him. I have not heard him. I have held on with white knuckles, and I've also let go.

Since Mary Magdalene and I have claimed each other in a way, I tell her these things. I ask her to pray. I tell her I can name the darkness, and this isn't it. Darkness is the spinning, the detachment from the body. The loss of my voice and my feet way above the ground. Darkness is when there is nothing to grasp to pull me back down or to pull me up out. It's the pit, and it's the too-wide open space beyond the sky. Darkness has no form, no direction.

Inside, gathered around the bar, the boys make plans to eat a hot pepper called the Carolina Reaper. It's the hottest pepper in the world, one that has measured in at 1,641,183 Scoville Heat Units. Because I live in a house with five Haines men who think eating hot peppers proves their masculinity, I have affectionately named this measurement the "Scrotum Heat Unit." I sit here laughing at my own wordplay while

13

being simultaneously furious that people I love can be such ding-dongs. Surely Mary knows the feeling.

The boys inside are not the only ones feeling the fire. The firepit is empty out here, but I can feel my fire. There's something beautiful about the mix of anger and laughter when you were once numb enough to have lost both. We're alive here on this half acre in the middle of town. Mouths are on fire, then soaked in milk. Petals twist back into their nightly fists. The beds uncrumple. Steam gathers on the dirty mirrors during showers. I am not healed. I ache all over, but this is not a dark place.

After a season of despair that so deeply threatened my body and mind, I feel like I might be glowing out here in the dark, and I tell my patroness as much. (Yes, sometimes I speak my inner thoughts to the saints. If they're still alive and praying, then I figure I may as well.) I smile, then walk toward the house, where I will give antacids and marching orders about brushing teeth.

This morning I bend to the coneflowers where their leaves have turned in the night from a deep-woods green to a composting brittle brown. Spiky black caterpillars hiding in the downturned foliage eat like they'll get to become silver checkerspot butterflies soon, but I don't care what they think they'll be. I care that they've rendered my Cheyenne Spirit coneflowers lifeless. I deadhead, pinch the brown petals from the top. I take it personally. I change my mind about having planted them for the butterflies, but this is still not a dark place. This is the feeling of choosing between life and death.

I stack a neat pile of leaves writhing with caterpillars to feed the chickens before I go around knocking squash bugs into a cup of soapy water. Sometimes I squish the bugs first because I'm still indifferent to their tiny lives. *I'm no St. Fran-*

cis, I tell Mary. *I'm no St. Clare either.* I am just Amber Haines, harbinger of death (at least to those tiny bugs). But I am also a way maker for the echinacea and cucumber vines.

The gothic sense of order this garden gives me is often in its show of life and death. It asks a lot of me but also shows me how so much of the work I've done hasn't mattered. It's a scene of love and interaction, and it's a scene for letting go too. There's not a thing alive here that something didn't die to make it so. There is nothing to eat that something didn't die to make it so. If I eat lettuce, it was at the expense of some munchy worm's life. That's the terrible news for all the vegans.

My garden is gorgeous when you stand back to see it, colorful, diverse, dying back and taking over at once, but when you stand up close, it's full of bite marks. The deer bit back every one of my okra and tomato plants. They bit into a habanero too but decided against it because even wild bucks don't measure their egos in Scrotum Heat Units. As it goes with all of life, things tend to look a little different with a magnifying glass: aphids, flea beetles, blossoms turned yellow and fallen to the ground before they got the chance to bloom.

Maybe this is why I'm drawn to it, the microcosm of a garden: because the work to temper critters and amend the soil is never done. I've been at it for years, and still, it seems at least once a week I learn something new that makes me want to slap my own face in awe or my forehead in stupidity. I fail constantly. I give up and murder a row of zucchini plants in a heated crime of passion, and then I turn around in the same minute to see a newly opened dahlia that makes me sing like I'm in my own musical. My garden is a romantic comedy and a murder mystery rolled into one. It morphs from day to day. Characters come in and go out. Nothing is boring. Nothing exists without pointing to or connecting with something else. Everything here turns lovely or gravely and often both.

I am surrounded by bees and moths that look like bees. There are daily hummingbirds and beans I cannot reach and flowers I forgot I planted until they bloom. There are ugly grubs that I dig out and smash with my boots on the rocks. I am no longer a vocational minister, but I'm finding similar work as a gardener. I plant seeds, water them, tend to the plants, make mistakes, make amends, root out what's rotten, and start over—all the things of ministry.

Again, this is not a dark place, but it isn't all light either. I have been somewhere in the gothic middle, where both life and death, the grotesque and the beautiful, shadow and light are at work. Learning the difference between these dichotomies over the past few years of recovery has been an exercise of trial and error. As I have fumbled to know the difference between light and dark, a truth has emerged in the darkest season of my life, but my eyes are still adjusting to it.

In my early days of vocational ministry, my priest and I traveled to an Anglican conference and stayed with a friend of mine who lives among orange and lemon trees. I remember being in the passenger's side of her car under the completely blue sky. I was thin back then and wore sunglasses as big as plates. I remember my priest telling me in front of my friend how he wanted me to take his job one day—these were his exact words: "Replace me." I was a better preacher and leader than he was, he said, and this wasn't the first time he'd heaped so much praise on me. But it was inspiring to hear him say it in front of a friend. He recognized the work I'd been doing in the church before he even got there, and he let me know that he saw me, kept me washed with awe that I could be so lucky to work with someone who could name my gifts, the gifts of a woman.

It was the carrot I needed after years of ministry as a writer and as a female lay leader. He made space for me. He called me a "minister," and his idealistic approach to women in ministry made him a champion in some circles. But things were odd. In one-on-one conversations, he said we should talk about how men and women working together should deal with their attractions. I told him Seth didn't like the language, but he said it was an important topic to discuss in the context of ministry between men and women, so I gave in. We were invited to share publicly about our work together, and he talked about how men and women can work in ministry relationships, even again, how they should deal with their attraction to one another. It felt as if the conversation had moved from being more general to being more specific to me, to him.

I believed he was the open door to my fulfilled life in ministry, but it didn't turn out to be light pouring in through that door. The shadows were engulfing. I started dressing in baggier clothes to be more unseen. I took copious notes with my head down at hours-long meetings where he instructed me to preach in his way, to no longer call him "brother" because "it means that we're close but not *that* close." Once, he told me, "We can't be afraid of erotic love, because then, what other types of love get cut off?" I wrote it word for word in my journal because it was just so confusing. Disorienting.

He never touched me, but near the end of my curacy, he told me we should talk about physical touch between friends. *No, thank you.* I assumed that ministry was just hard, especially as a woman in a man's world. Everyone says that, so I kept that death grip on what I thought was the light and the role I could play in being a light in this dark world. But it was getting darker inside those church walls, and I stood and watched it, paralyzed by false hope.

The final flick of the light switch was when I didn't recognize my voice anymore. I couldn't find it for anything, especially in church, and wasn't it my job to speak? That's when I wrote a long letter to my dearest friends and fellow church leaders sharing my experience and asking them to help protect me, because I didn't want to talk about being *that* close with the priest or erotic love or physical touch or any of it anymore. But the church isn't always the best at protecting its women. Mary Magdalene knows. At the very least, she witnessed Jesus's ministry to the women who had many stones aimed at them.

Looking back, I see that the brightness of the promise of a beautiful future was blinding. It was the invitation into C. S. Lewis's "The Inner Ring,"[6] acceptance into the fraternity of ministry that would allow me to *use my gifts* if I'd just go along with the one in power. It was such a bright promise made by someone in that inner ring, and I couldn't see how long and dark the shadows were becoming until they swallowed up the carrot he dangled. They swallowed me up too. This is how I learned to let go. I simply couldn't see the carrot or myself anymore.

These years later, I'm not an Anglican curate but a lay Roman Catholic with no formal place of ministry. The internal work required to make such a transition often happened in my garden while I considered Mary Magdalene, who witnessed an insane amount of transformation in the garden. She's taught me it takes time for the eyes to adjust to the light.

Today, looking at one of those enormous boulders, I remember the Sunday after Jesus's death, when Mary walked to the tomb and saw a rock rolled from its mouth. She went in and couldn't find him. She turned desperate, frantic in the search for the one who loved her the very most. She was ready to take his body to wash and care for it and had come to the garden, willing to do the work. The only person she found (who wasn't robed in crisp angel white) was a man she assumed was the gardener (John 20:15). He must have been dingy, maybe not so bright. Maybe he had a fistful of herbs and had wiped his other hand across his clothes. Mary begged him to tell her where to find Jesus. It must have been dark, because she couldn't see him for who he was.

I can't imagine the care she brought to the garden for the one who had spoken her name. He didn't assign her a place based on her body, a worth based on what good light she could shine on him. He simply knew *her*. Mary. The gardener spoke her name, but he wasn't just a gardener. He was the Gardener, and in that moment she saw him and, in so doing, became the apostle to the apostles. She ran back and spoke the good news for the very first time to the men who were hiding in despair: *The tomb is not a dark place. He is risen!*

Most Christians know this, how there's rarely a gospel scene without women, how especially the resurrection shows a woman's role in proclamation. It blows my mind in the way a seed cracks open and bursts out with root and stem. The first sighting of the resurrected Lord was one where he revealed himself to a woman in his creation overalls. It wasn't just Jesus in a new body, risen and showing he had defeated death. He was Creator God, who had hovered over the void with his potter hands, and he knew that Mary knew the void.

Are there words for that kind of darkness, that void? We know there aren't. Words don't exist there. The darkness consumes everything in it. What is left of us in that void? What could ever break into it? Only the one who is the word, the verb, *Love*. He's the one Word from the beginning, and across the void, he knew Mary. And he knows me. We have seen his garden side, his dirty Eden hands. The tomb, empty of false hope, false light. I would never pretend to know Mary's real story, her demons, but I'll never stop being grateful that she's still teaching us that we can sit in the dark because there's one who comes to meet, name, and resurrect us there.

There's no way to count the deep down things in a garden, all the tiny lives and deaths and true beauties that connect us with God, whom I often call the Divine Love. God meeting his people in the garden—it's an ancient story. The one of Adam and Eve walking in the cool of the evening with God? Yes. But also, it's Mary's story, the one of a despairing woman who encounters life, even after death.

There have been stories all along of people who experienced the Divine Love who transformed their lives, and we call these people saints. Some are "Saints" in the proper sense, meaning some folks in Rome got together and convinced the pope that the lives of those holy men and women were worthy of formal canonization. (You'll meet a few of those saints in this book.) There are other saints, though, saints like those Coptic martyrs who gave their lives for their faith on the beaches of Egypt in 2015, a story I still think about from time to time. There are everyday saints, like the Church of Christ women who prayed for me in my high school years, when I was wandering around, lost as a goose. There are saints like Seth's granny, who read her Bible under a magnifying glass in her last lucid years, or like my mamaw, whose long-suffering could draw the sweetness out of the meanest soul. These saints remind us that even though it seems like the pitch of night, this world is no dark place. In the stories of the saints, I find that I'm not so different from the ones who've come and gone before me. All of us human, all of us in and out of the dark, all of us searching for a love to know us. All of us given the chance to see love taking shape before our eyes.

I didn't grow hope in a vacuum, just as I've never grown a garden in a vacuum. Things take time to break down and break open. In my darkest days, I grew hope by pressing into the ancient stories. I followed the thread of love stretching from Mary Magdalene's life, through the lives of the saints, and down into mine. There I found the very real Christ, an actual-factual living hope who shows himself to us everywhere and in all the deep down things but also in the very real stuff of our lives. If only we have the eyes to see.

Practice: Pick a Patron Saint

In the south transept of the Chartres Cathedral in France, the four evangelists—Matthew, Mark, Luke, and John—are shown sitting atop the shoulders of the major prophets—Isaiah, Jeremiah, Ezekiel, and Daniel. The imagery is fitting for this particular cathedral. As Joseph Pearce writes, "According to John of Salisbury, writing in 1159, 'Bernard of Chartres used to say that we are like dwarfs on the shoulders of giants, so that we can see more than they, and things at a greater distance, not by virtue of any sharpness of sight on our part, or any physical distinction, but because we are carried high and raised up by their giant size.'"[7]

Across Christian history, other giants have emerged—Hopkins, Mary Magdalene, Augustine, Francis of Assisi, Clare of Assisi, Mother Teresa, Dorothy Day, and so many others. The author of the biblical book of Hebrews calls this the "great cloud of witnesses" (12:1), and so many of them earned their sainthood by perseverance through persecution or by tending to the outcasts of society. If we get to know them, if we sit on their shoulders, we might learn a thing or two about what it means to carry hope in poverty, persecution, depression, doubt, or other times of despair.

Pick a saint from Christian history. Get to know them. As you study, take note: What despair did they face, and how did they meet hope in the face of it? Then let their life speak to yours.

If you don't know where to start in Christian history, identify someone in your life you consider an example of truth, beauty, and goodness. What makes their life so beautiful to you? How can you follow in their footsteps, their example? Make a list and be specific.

two

TELL THE STORY

Seth: Choose Your Attachments

This is how I remember falling in love. It was sweater weather just before the front moved in, before the temperature plummeted and sleet pelted us at the intramural football fields. I'd made a roommate promise—I'd watch Billy Neal play at least one club game that year—so I showed up, because promises between roommates are the closest thing to a vow a college student can make. Amber had made no such promise, but she met me at the fields anyway, wearing those comfortable jeans with the holes above the knee and the brown jacket that snugged up around her waist, so it'd be a lie to say I was paying attention to Billy at all. There are more important things than football.

She was going on about the Pixies or PJ Harvey or some other grunge-era artist she loved in that transcendent musical era of American history, and then the air shifted. Thin mist gathered and turned to ice pellets as the temperature bottomed out, how it sometimes does in an Ozark autumn. It was a convenient excuse to seek shelter.

The half-mile walk from the fields to the coffee shop should have been a miserable, stinging jaunt. Tiny ice pelted us, crystallized in her "boggin," which she said was Appalachian vernacular for a stocking cap. We found the last available table—the one in the back by the couch, where the gross couples used to sit on each other's laps—and she shook the ice out of her hat while I brushed it out of my hair. There we shared liquid conversation, moving from music, to childhood, to spirituality, and back to music. At that table, she shared enough to let me know she'd done a fair bit of wandering from faith, first through the kind of musical artists she loved but then more explicitly.

"I'm still a smoker," she said, though she admitted she hadn't smoked in a handful of weeks. Then she added that if good faith required her to dress up, play a part, and repeat the proper answers to every question, she'd have none of it. It wasn't her way, and that's why she'd done what so many kids raised on the Bible and Kurt Cobain did in the '90s. She ran.

If she'd have known that all that running would lead her to become a full-on believer—a Christian minister, for God's sake—would she have ever started running in the first place? Would she have seen the irony in this kind of future and simply given up and given in to the grace that imbued the very air she breathed? Would she have stopped running in Alabama and settled into a faith closer to her homeplace? I don't know because that's not how the story went.

Just weeks before, she'd crumpled on her dorm-room floor, all burned out from so much running and certain death had come for her. She looked into the mirror and didn't recognize herself. *Recognize*—this was the word she used. Was it the thinning frame or the sunken eyes or just the shape of a life that she'd sort of fallen into? I still wonder why she used that word, why she still uses it today. How does a woman forget her features?

That conversation in that coffee shop was the first time she invoked Mary Magdalene, I think, though time does things to stories, makes them a bit cleaner and more connected than they were. Still, this is how I remember it: she didn't just identify with Mary; she *was* Mary, or at least the version of her that came of age in a decade of guitar distortion, baggy sweaters, and jeans with threadbare knees. And while she was on that floor, hopeless in her lack of recognition, she heard a voice or felt a sort of knowing from God: "I will never love you more than I love you right now." It was the moment the Divine Love recognized her, in her lowest moment, and she recognized the simplest hope: if she was already loved in her state of grief and confusion and disorder, then maybe she could live as if she were loved. So, she got up. She chose life over death.

Recognize. That word. Back then, I might have been more prone to use the word *saved*, because that's the thing the Baptists I was raised around were so preoccupied with. In our present, more Catholic context, maybe I'd lean toward *converted*. I'm not sure those words do justice to her experience, really. I think *recognize* fits the bill.

Recognize. What's in the word? It is a verb, a word of action that means to remember something when you see it. We recognize each of our kids in their baby pictures but also now in their man-sized bodies. We recognized our friends Joseph and Lindsey when they came home from four long years in Indonesia. We recognize the patterns and movements of the Mass, whether it's offered in English, Spanish, or Italian. *Recognize* is a word that has intimate connotations. We recognize what we've lived with, engaged, hugged, kissed, ingested, whatever.

That is what I've understood was the truth of Amber's experience. When she no longer knew herself, the Divine Love saw her, knew her and all the versions of herself she'd

25

been and would be. Mary Amber was kin with Mary Magdalene. She was both loved and given the hope that she could continue to live in that love.

On that sleet-covered November night, I recognized something too: *love*. Not love as an intellectual construct or a theological idea. Not the abstracted love that might save me from my sins and seat me in the heavenly places to rule and reign and yada, yada, yada. Instead, I recognized a woman so possessed by her encounter with the Divine Love that she rose up from the floor, more fully herself, ready to live for the first time.

My God, that's a glorious thing.

I've come to know this truth: there will be times when you do not recognize yourself. By degrees, over days, weeks, months, you lose track of your features. You avoid any mirror, any reflection because you know what you see will be something other.

In 2013, in the stone-cold lobby of a Methodist church in Austin, Texas, the world tilted. Up and down, left and right, an easy seasickness. The souring smell of the previous night's tequila hung there, just behind my nostrils, overpowering the coffee in my cup and the breakfast tacos I'd scarfed in an attempt to push away my hangover and steel my legs. Across the cold tile floor of the dim foyer, the lobby doors opened, and a woman entered the room through a thousand shards of light. As the doors closed and my eyes adjusted, the silhouette took shape, and there she was. Heather. A recovering alcoholic and friend. As she smiled her hello, I heard something like a warning somewhere in my skull: "You can either deal with this now, or things will get bad."

This was the closest thing I'd ever heard to the voice of God, at least that's how I sorted it out in the moment, and so I crossed the lobby and put it to her straight: "How did you know you had a drinking problem?" That question was an epiphany. I already knew.

This is the anatomy of a drinking problem: take a human; fill them with pain or crisis or anxiety; tell them it's an existential pain, an endless one; hand them a bottle; see the bottle take the shape of a doctor, lover, friend, anyone who can take away pain for a moment; watch the relationship grow singular, demanding, problematic, abusive; see the human deny the abuse, refuse to call the thing a thing. Alcoholism? Anything but that. I'd have preferred to name it Stockholm Syndrome. You love the thing that treats you like shit.

It had been a season of touch-and-go health for our youngest son, Titus. A year earlier, he'd been hospitalized for over a month. There were veiled death threats by mother nature or father time or whoever was responsible for his sickness. When he was released, a team of doctors monitored his progress as we wrestled with feeding tubes, shelled out the big bucks for elemental formula, and prayed for resolution, and if not resolution, then answers—*why wasn't our son thriving?* And when neither resolution nor answers came, when all the prayers failed to achieve any sort of eternal orbit, when my boyhood belief in a God who gave a damn about me failed, I made a calculated decision: I'd quit him, and I'd do it without praying. I'd turn to my abuser—whiskey, gin, Jägermeister, whatever—and let it wash me into an icy numbness. And for just over a year, that's what I did.

There was a bottle in my desk drawer at work, and that bottle came out a little earlier every day. There were happy hours with clients too, and one suggested I buy a membership to Ben's Apartment, the speakeasy behind the cigarette machine in the dance club, because it was the cool place to drink. I poured doubles at home, sometimes triples. Who knew? No one, because God wound a special gift into my

DNA—the ability to handle liquor like a Welsh warlord. But in my Methodist-lobby epiphany in 2013, I saw the truth in a sort of mirror—the face of my friend Heather. And once I saw it, I couldn't unsee it. I had a by God, bona fide drinking problem.

Now here's the truth about real southern gentlemen with bona fide drinking problems: they are levees. They hold back rivers of anxiety, often with a little help from Jack or Johnnie or Evan or Jose. But take away the bottle, and the levee breaks, and that's when the anxieties behind their eyes come rushing in. In just such a moment, afraid of drowning in the flood of sheer terror—terror about Titus, work, whatever—I would surely discover in sobriety, I called a local therapist, who, after I shared the news that I'd broken up with the bottle, said, "The bad news is you're bad enough off to come see me; the good news is I'm free tomorrow at noon." And that's how my weekly lunch-hour therapy appointments started.

Week after week, he led me through my own tangled psychology, from the easy days of my thin boyhood faith to the days of present pain. Some things are more certain than death and taxes, he said, and among those? Pain. He taught me the wisdom of Rumi—the cure for the pain is the pain—and he showed me that healing requires dealing and dealing wouldn't happen as long as I numbed everything with booze. The only problem? Feeling pain hurts like hell. In all that feeling, I wondered, where was God? Was God, even? If he was, was he absent? Or worse, capricious?

I set out to feel because I figured I didn't have much else to lose, and in that journey, two very important things happened.

Thing 1: I dedicated a chair in my living room to my search for God, and one night, while I was trying not to hurl curses at the God who I was told existed somewhere above the ceiling, a simple prayer came to mind. It was a prayer I once heard from a Franciscan brother: "Lord Jesus Christ, Son of God, have mercy on me, a sinner." That prayer—taken directly from Scripture—had been prayed by the Eastern Orthodox for centuries, often while thumbing their fingers across knotty rosaries. It was direct and simple, a request that Christ would do what he'd done for over two thousand years: make space for the returning idiot. (That idiot was me.) As I considered that prayer, as I rolled it around in my noggin and on my lips, it became my own.

Thing 2: Over one of our noon-hour sessions, my very good counselor shared the work of noted marriage therapist Sue Johnson, who specializes in "emotionally focused therapy." He asked me to spend time with her via YouTube, outing a hunch that there might be something for me in her videos. And so I returned to my office, shut the door, and pulled up the link he'd texted as I left his office.

I listened as Johnson said in a dry British accent, "Effective dependency makes us stronger as individuals." She explained that those with a bonded marital attachment were better able to define themselves in more positive terms, better able to regulate their emotions, better able to navigate the worst the world has to offer. At least, that's what the scientific research showed.

"Bonded attachment"—the phrase grabbed me. If healthy, bonded attachment to another person increased the chances of negotiating the pains of life, could there be some spiritual corollary? Could any "human, merely being," as E. E. Cummings wrote,[1] connect with the unimaginable divine being? It was a question worthy of asking because, after all, I was a Christian, even if a drunk one, and so I scoured the internet for some spiritual guru who'd written about attachment and addiction, and one name kept rising to the top of the search results: St. Ignatius of Loyola.

Now, despite my years in Catholic school, despite my affinity for their crucifixes, saints, and incense, I was still 98 percent Protestant. (I had always reserved 2 percent for a more Catholic possibility.) I knew nothing about St. Ignatius other than he was some Catholic dead dude who, up to that point, had no relevance to my life. But as I read his story, I found myself in it.

In St. Ignatius's own words, he was "enthralled by the vanities of the world" before his conversion.[2] But after a battlefield wound, the sixteenth-century Spaniard found himself laid up in a makeshift hospital room, which boasted a spartan, two-book library. One book was on the life of Christ, the other about the lives of the saints. As he read, he was recognized by the same love that recognized Mary Magdalene, Peter, Paul, and all the saints down through history. And in that recognition, his vain appetites gave way to something more holy: he found himself longing for sainthood.

Ignatius began attending daily Mass and tempering his appetites for food, drink, wealth, and glory. He cultivated his own bonded attachment—*affection* was the word he used—but not to a spouse. Instead, he attached himself to the divine love of God through Christ, and he treated everything else as secondary.

Divine attachment became Ignatius's gateway for mercy, and it led to perhaps the greatest work of Christian spiritual formation: *The Spiritual Exercises*. The exercises, he said, were a method for "preparing and disposing the soul to rid itself of all inordinate attachments, and, after their removal, of seeking and finding the will of God in the disposition of our life for the salvation of our soul."[3] *Inordinate attachments*—like booze?

In the months following my discovery of St. Ignatius, I pored over *The Spiritual Exercises*. I began meeting with an Ignatian spiritual director to help me understand Ignatius's notion of attachment to God and detachment from the vices of life. As I did, I discovered a new way of imaginative prayer, one that helped me cultivate a less anxious, less nerves-on-fire kind of sobriety, one that helped me understand that I was recognized by God's love. That way of praying came directly from Ignatius's writings on food and wine.

Pretty fitting, eh?

Ignatius knew that food and wine might lead to "disordered attachments," or addiction. So the good saint offered a practical prayer exercise to bring all things into their proper order. He wrote, "While one is eating, let him imagine he sees Christ our Lord and His disciples at table, and consider how He eats and drinks, how He looks, how He speaks, and then strive to imitate Him. In this way, his mind will be occupied principally with our Lord, and less with the provision for the body. Thus he will come to greater harmony and order in the way he ought to conduct himself."[4]

The advice was as simple as it was profound. When the chaos came calling—and I knew it would—when I was tempted to turn to the bottle, I was to imagine Christ in the room and ask whether he'd pick up that bottle to deal with the pain. If he wouldn't, then I shouldn't either. And in those moments of pain, I'd pull a set of prayer beads from my pocket and run my thumbs over the smooth stones as I prayed, "Lord Jesus Christ, Son of God, have mercy on me, a sinner." I'd pray the prayer imagining Christ in the room with me, him recognizing me in my pain. Somehow, in that imaginative prayer, the anxiety passed.

Through this imaginative prayer practice, I began to learn a deep down thing: every moment is an ordained opportunity, even the painful ones. In time and space, we can choose to connect with the Creator of the cosmos instead of the things that fill that cosmos. As I did that very thing, I began to see that created gifts—things like wine, food, sex, or whatever—comprise the good stuff, made good by the goodness of God, and they can be portals of connection to the divine if we order them under his creative love. But if we use these gifts as ends in themselves, as ways of numbing pain, then addiction is the natural result.

I've been walking this path of ordering—and constantly reordering—attachments for almost a decade. As I have, I've found myself following the advice of St. Ignatius. He led me through those early years of shaky sobriety. He led me into an imaginative prayer practice that deepens my bonded attachment to the Divine Love, which I've come to believe is the only path to true sobriety. And I've learned that all the good things of the earth are meant to be enjoyed in proper relation to the Christ who created them. This is the mercy of the deep down thing.

Quitting ain't easy because when the pain comes calling, everything feels so damned demented. The chaos of a soul distorts your reflection, brings that pain that begs you to reach for anything to soothe it. But here's what I know, both from Amber's story and from my own: In the darkest days of despair, Christ meets us on dorm-room floors and in Methodist church lobbies. He comes and says, "I see you; I recognize you; let's get up and choose a different way." And as we choose and choose and choose, day after day, ordained moment after ordained moment, we begin to recognize our true selves again.

Amber: Body Talk

I used to be a fighter. An example of this is the time Seth left with the boys to take them to school. I was in my nightgown, watching the sunrise through the back door, when a man walked out of our tool shed with a hatchet. Somehow, at that moment, it didn't register that this could turn into a very murdery morning for me. Instead, I opened the sliding glass door with almost zero clothes on and tromped barefooted through my yard to the stranger-man who had begun throwing said hatchet into the air and catching it by the handle. I asked him what he was doing in my stuff, seemingly without an ounce of fear, but the truth is it was fear pulsing through my brain that pushed me out that door. He told me that he was homeless and in the churchyard next door with some friends. He wasn't in his right mind and had been rummaging through the shed for supplies. As I walked back to the house to put on clothes and grab them a little food, I started shaking. What was I thinking? Maybe I wasn't, but my body sure did go out there to claim my hatchet, didn't it?

In moments of stress, when the amygdala kicks in and sends us into fight, flight, fawn, or freeze mode, our brains don't give us a multiple-choice questionnaire to see which survival option we'd like best in the moment. My body has sent me out the back door ready to pick a fight with a stranger wielding a hatchet. It's also sent me fawning in agreement with things I didn't like or want in order to keep me safe too. I'm sure I've taken flight in ways that seem perfectly reasonable to me, though I can't remember a particular instance. It's the freezing that has been the hardest to sort because it involves inactivity. It's the opposite of who I know myself to be. I don't freeze. I do something, even if that something is to walk myself out near naked on a platter to a potential murder person while I'm home alone.

If I was an icon of anything in the months after my curacy ended, then I'm afraid it was the icon of one curled in bed asking why she couldn't move. Why was I so frozen? I gave myself lashes over it—believe me—but the truth is that even in bed, I wasn't devoid of hope because I had been frozen in despair before. I remembered what it was like not to recognize myself in the mirror and not to know what to do but lie down on a linoleum floor in my dorm room and give in to the despair. I remembered Jesus. I hadn't invited him there because I didn't know to, but there he was, present to pain, and I had to make a choice to believe the love that met me there. I recognized and believed Jesus then, and I recognized him still, even in my frozen state. I had to allow myself to stay in bed until the noise of my own whip quietened down enough for me to experience that love again.

Back when Seth called from a conference in Austin to tell me he had to give up drinking, I wasn't as familiar with the language of survival as I am now, how the body always has something to say to us when we're in survival mode or dealing with intense fear or loss. I did recognize fear in his voice, though, the question of whether he'd make it or not, because we had endured almost losing our baby together and knew that familiar rush of despair. He told me to get rid of every drop of alcohol, so I called our friend Jared, who didn't waste a minute driving to the house and who was grateful for the haul of gin, whiskey, and beer he inherited. I assumed that changing a drinking habit would be hard, but I wasn't experienced enough to understand what was about to happen. Seth had no choice but to feel it. *All of it.* And by *all of it*, I mean all the emotions—the anxiety, the worry, the sadness, the pain. In his dedicated chair, I watched him unbox himself again and again like a matryoshka doll of stories. Inside one grief were a hundred others.

Another way to put it is this: grief is a river and one where all griefs seem to coalesce. When we fall in that river, it can feel sort of like drowning or thrashing through white waters, slamming into the painful edges of other losses, and all in a panic to keep the nose above the water because there's no-where to set the feet. The river of grief is a complex moving body where so many things coexist. It can even harbor beauty or level out with some stillness we didn't know we could find.

Years later, when we thought we knew things about grief and sobriety, the waters rose again. When Seth quit leading worship and I quit my work as curate and stepped out of the ordination process to get away from the priest, our fellow church planters and dear friends reached out to us for a very clear answer as to why we were pulling away as leaders. We wanted to do what it took to keep our heads above the water, to avoid falling into the river of grief if we could. I wrote out the details and fought to help them understand the shape of things. We put it all there, in letter format, hoping the church community and the bishop of the diocese would get it. Then, we waited.

And waited.

And waited.

The news came down. Our bishop asked our friends to wait to share our story with other leaders. Meanwhile, the priest filled the pulpit, preached sermons, and led vestry meetings. Maybe that's when we fell into the river of grief.

A "third party" came to evaluate our church and my circumstance. The third party issued a report, and that report contained insinuations. Did I enjoy it when he crossed the boundaries, maybe even a little? The river of grief rose up to my chin.

Weeks passed, and the report wasn't shared with the congregation. In fact, nothing was. The river rose over my mouth.

Our friends announced from the pulpit that they had decided (along with the priest) that he would no longer be our leader (not that he was fired), that they were sending him out with hope and grace. And when they asked the congregation to find ways to love him well as his family transitioned away over another month without any mention of my experience (or any mention of others' experiences of pain at the church), I went all the way under.

Had the church protected anyone but him? It couldn't be called abuse (not even emotional or spiritual), they said, because there was *no way to prove he meant to do it*. Frequency? Doesn't matter. Narrative spinning with other church members? Who cares. The other members who had already left the congregation citing similar reasons, albeit without the sexual connotations? Bygones and all of that. Sure, he was dismissive, manipulative, and controlling narratives, but they couldn't prove he intended any of it because *who can really judge a man's heart?* And so, his story prevailed, even as he "stepped away from" his job. Even as I write, he has another job in ministry, one where people either don't know his history or pretend it doesn't exist.

There are times when his name pops up, and there I sense the white waters rising. I don't know if this is what it means to be triggered, but I know what it means to feel like drowning in the river of grief. And there, in those waters, it's amazing what we find. There, old histories come back. There, I slide headlong into the memory of holding our baby as we thought he was dying. There, I question my identity like I did during my parents' divorce. There, I miss the aunt I had assumed would guide me all my life. There, my body feels the weight of every grief I've ever experienced.

Even now, when I write or speak my story, I feel swept up in the river because writing it is what I did to ask for help from the people I trusted most. I was dismissed, and the ground washed out from beneath my feet. When I'm swept up, I have a hard time hearing my own strong voice, which means I find it easier and easier to not recognize myself anymore. And in that lack of recognition, there I go, flailing up and down in the river.

Who's to say how to keep from falling back into the river of grief or how to get out once we're there? I don't think it's as easy as just asking Jesus to pull us out because, as best I can tell, he didn't save himself from his own river of grief. Were there a formula, I'd sell it to you and the rest of the world, and I'd use the money to buy a bunch of shoes and handbags, and I'd buy Seth every guitar he ever wanted. Really, I would.

So often, we don't choose to get in or out of the river. We don't choose to grieve or not. Grief is tautological—it is what it is. It's a hunter. It finds us. The question is what does it mean to live our one life in the midst of such pain? How can we keep going, especially when there's no immediate relief, vindication, or justice? Will we stop thrashing long enough to remember who we are, to realize that even though we're in pain, we are not our pain? We are something beyond the thrashing, the numb emotions in the icy waves.

Somewhere along the way I remembered this. I remembered that it was the Divine Love who pulled me up from the floor, from my first river of grief. It was the Divine Love who recognized me and helped me recognize myself. It was the Divine Love who showed me my next move, and that move was simply to learn to receive God's love.

Seth asks, "How does a woman forget her features?" Even now, as I struggle to write, I keep thinking of St. James, who says, "For if any are hearers of the word and not doers, they are like those who look at themselves in a mirror; for they look at themselves and, on going away, immediately forget what they were like" (James 1:23–24 NRSV). I've experienced this time and again. I forget my own face, what I know to be true and who I know myself to be, especially when the grief sets in. But when I remember that even Christ had his own grief and that God's love animated him even in that grief, I know the river won't drown me. I know I can get up, move forward, just like he did. I know the truth of my body can line up with the truth of what I believe. I know I can find something like resurrection.

We act in accordance with hope, and hope believes that love moves us through grief. We're headed somewhere. The river isn't all there is. Even if not immediately, love will bring us justice, peace, and vindication, and when we open our eyes to the truth that love is wider than the river of grief, we can move toward the mirror and recognize ourselves again. In that recognition—that love—we can move forward, in spite of the river.

Practice: Create a Lifeline

None of us set out to fall into the river of grief. Grief simply happens. It's a fact of life. In this book, we've set out to help you navigate your way through that river with hope-filled, grounded, tangible, deep-down-thing practices.

We don't know much, but we know that love is the promise that gives us hope in despair. That's why we reflect on our early days of falling in love, why Seth stays close to those moments when he experienced attachment to the Divine Love in the newness of sobriety, why Amber carries the memory of God recognizing her on her dorm-room floor. When we stay close to the ways we've experienced the Divine Love holding us up, pushing us forward, helping us navigate, it gives us hope that it will happen again.

As writers, we believe there is power in the written word. (Like Hopkins, we believe that writing is a deep down thing.) Set aside thirty minutes with a pencil and a sheet of paper. On that paper, create a lifeline—a time line of your life that marks the moments you experienced the Divine Love. Write two or three sentences about each moment, then keep the time line close to your bedside. Review it in the morning when you wake up and in the evening when you go to sleep. Add to the list as you experience new moments of the Divine Love. If you're in a season of despair (or when you enter a new and difficult season), ask the Divine Love to show up as the Divine Love has shown up in the past.

three

FIND GOD IN THE STUFF OF EARTH

Seth: Go to the River, the Trail, the Chapel

It's a two-mile climb from the parking lot to the top of Mount Kessler. From my car, I cross the stream to a muddy bank, slog through to the meadow before the climb. There's a soft rain falling, pelting the splayed petals of a thousand will-be blackberries. Those flowers remind me of starfish somehow, and they dance in the air when the rain falls on their centers.

Today is a longer run, an exorcism as much as an exercise. It's twelve miles of wildflowers, stream crossings, hilly switchbacks, muddy landings, and trail crossings so confusing that I run with my iPhone to make sure I don't accidentally end up running to Oklahoma. This is the place where I come to turn off the world so that I can make sense of it. And it's been a season when there's been so much to make sense of, like, *What does it mean to be the one who carries hope?* or *What does it mean that some choose not to?*

It's been no easy thing carrying hope, particularly because the world seems hell-bent on burning it all down. In the last half decade, we watched on television as the world went up in flames. Forest fires. The melting of the polar ice caps. The burning of the cathedral of Notre-Dame, a monument to Christ that stood for almost eight centuries. A global pandemic. The precinct in Minnesota that burned to the ground after George Floyd's murder. The city streets around our country engulfed in flames and tear gas. The cities of Ukraine turned to smoking cinder. Politics has been its own smoldering Gehenna (God bless the USA). And besides all this, who can say what other fires might erupt in the space between starting this sentence and punctuating it?

I've watched so much fire in the last five years that when I stop to read my trail map, I imagine all of Mount Kessler on fire, and not the autumnal fire of maple leaves but an actual forest fire with flames dancing in the canopy. This year was supposed to be different.

In December, I declared 2021 "The Year of Hope" in a sort of Osteenian prosperity gamble. There was reason for hope. The acrimonious election was over. COVID vaccines were in production, so herd immunity was just around the corner. The economy was rebooting, and my work was picking back up. In just a few months, I'd be back with the old crew at Puritan—Abby, Masie, Jonathon.

Yes, the year of hope was upon us.

It lasted six days.

On January 6, the New Year leaned over to 2020 and said, "Hold my beer," then commenced to instigate an American insurrection, which produced, among other things, chants to hang the vice president. But the New Year didn't stop there. It suggested the pandemic virus reinvent itself and gave us the Delta variant, which was magnitudes more contagious and swept across India, then the United Kingdom, then the

United States. A snowpocalypse spread across the south, threatening the power grid of the state of Texas. Six Asian American women were murdered in a mass shooting in Atlanta, and less than a week later, another ten people were killed in a mass shooting in a supermarket in Boulder, Colorado. All of this happened in just the first one hundred days.

The year of our Lord 2021—if ever we felt we needed a respite year, this was it. Instead, it was another self-immolating year in a series of self-immolating years.

Certain of my route, I peel to the right, winding up a trail called "Serpentine." The trail snakes along the northern side of the ridge before dropping onto "Egg Beater," the snake giving way to the scrambler. It is apropos of everything that is 2021.

The global events were bad enough, and they exposed plenty of reasons for despair—political violence caused by disinformation, the plight of the poor who suffered under winter weather and lack of access to medical care, the continuing systems of racism that kill humans made in God's image. It was the continuation of the human drama, one that'd been going on since the first humans ate that forbidden fruit. None of it should have come as a surprise because, as the writers of *Battlestar Galactica* put it, "All of this has happened before, and all this will happen again." Still, my waning hope wasn't the product of the world's cycle of chaos. My hope was threatened by something closer to home.

In April, we lost a friend to despair and a bullet. He was an avid outdoorsman, a hiker, someone who knew the Kessler trails "Serpentine" and "Eggbeater" and "Crazy Mary" and "Chinkapin Oak." He often came to the woods to be alone, to sort out the world. Maybe like Thoreau, he "never found the companion that was so companionable as solitude."[1] But somewhere along the way, he found no solace anywhere, not even in the solitude of Kessler. He fell asleep to hope, and that's how death won.

I'd just finished dressing for the Good Friday Mass when I received the call, and there, something like black ink filled me. After hanging up, I told Amber, and her face contorted in confusion and tears. My face was stony and blank, my body numb. This was the day two thousand years ago that despair took shape and drove a nail through hope's hands. It was the day two thousand years later that I lost my friend.

That night, as I sat through the Good Friday service, all I could seem to get out was, "My God, my God, where in the world have you gone?" This, I think, is the crux of despair. It is the moment when the black ink comes, when it does not simply hide the sun but snuffs it out altogether.

In this year of fire and black ink, I've thought a lot about that friend. I wish he would have been better acquainted with St. Ignatius, the saint who knew what it meant to overcome, even with a suffering psyche.

This is the part I haven't shared about Ignatius, the part I don't like thinking about. Even after his conversion, after his decision to follow Christ and become a saint, he still suffered. Conversion might save the soul, but it doesn't always lead to immediate relief and joy, no matter what the holy rollers say. (And the holy rollers say a lot . . . you know?) When Ignatius left that hospital in fresh faith, he was still filled with deep sadness, the black ink, and he set out on a pilgrimage, believing that walking toward God would somehow give him some relief. Ignatius stopped at a monastery, confessed his sins, and hung up his sword before the Black Madonna of Montserrat. He made his way to the village of Manresa, volunteered at a hospital, and adopted the life of a mendicant. He spent hours a day praying in a cave, where he no doubt practiced self-mortification, just like the other holy men and women of the day. Still, he couldn't shake the continuing humiliation of his bum leg, the depression and despair of his simple life, the suicidal ideation that had, by that time, attached itself to him as a noose.

Ignatius knew the feeling of the sun being snuffed out. He saw his disability as a reminder of it.

I make the turn to a short uphill segment called "Spellbound." I could walk this section, but then again, my legs work just fine, and a downhill segment is coming, my favorite segment, "Chinkapin Oak." So I keep running.

Saints aren't made by mere effort, I don't think. There's effort involved, sure, but isn't it the connection of effort and some miracle that creates the shapes of saints? Isn't it a sort of divine both-and?

Months into his stint at Manresa, months into prayer and fasting and mortification and almsgiving and services, while praying at the Cardoner River, Ignatius reached up and up and up, begging for relief, and that's when the vision came. It was so outside himself, he wrote of the experience in a third-person narrative:

> He sat down for a little while with his face to the river— Cardoner—which was running deep. While he was seated there, the eyes of his understanding began to be opened; though he did not see any vision, he understood and knew many things, both spiritual things and matters of faith and learning, and this was with so great an enlightenment that everything seemed new to him. It was as if he were a new man with a new intellect.[2]

Ignatius went to the river to beg for relief from that black ink, and there the Divine Love opened his heart and pulled him from his own river of grief. For the rest of his life, he ran after the Divine Love that reorders a life, even when new griefs came calling.

The Spanish saint wrote of his hope in "Contemplation to Attain Love," found in *The Spiritual Exercises*. He begins by describing love:

> Love consists in a mutual sharing of goods, for example, the lover gives and shares with the beloved what he possesses, or something of that which he has or is able to give; and vice versa, the beloved shares with the lover. Hence, if one has knowledge, he shares it with the one who does not possess it; and so also if one has honors, or riches. Thus, one always gives to the other.[3]

His explanation of love borders on clinical, but when you strip away the semiformal language, there's beauty in that diamond. Lovers demonstrate their love by way of giving. They give time, effort, consolation, sure. But they also give the tangible stuff of earth—flowers, bottles of champagne, fine leather goods. And wasn't this true of God?

In his "Contemplation to Attain Love," Ignatius isn't suggesting that his followers follow some daily gratitude journal prompt, though that might be helpful for some. Instead, he walks us into a fundamentally deeper practice, the practice of seeing the love of God in all the gifts of the whole wide world—the gifts of friendship, food, wine, sex, babies, music, poetry, art, literature, everything.

I pound down the switchbacks on "Chinkapin Oak," splashing through puddles, sliding in the soft spots on the trail. As I do, I think about the family my friend left behind, a group of people who are likely having difficulty finding any gifts of love in the world around them. I think about Amber too, how every gift must have felt hollow when she was in the depths of that river of grief. I think about the Asian community who lost its sisters, the Boulder community who lost its neighbors, the Black community who loses its sons

45

year after year. It is not easy to recognize the gifts of God in a world so full of sorrow. I pray for some relief for all of them. My prayers are simple when I run.

I come to the end of the trail, and the sun breaks through the clouds and the tree canopy. The raindrops falling from that canopy catch the sun and fill with tiny rainbows. A few steps down the path, I stop because two box turtles have used the break in the rain to come out and play. They're getting frisky, and they don't care that I'm standing directly over them. The enormity of death and life and darkness and light all converges right here, and I catch myself laughing at two turtles making turtle babies. Surrounded by the gifts of God's love, I know something true.

This is why I run the trails. There, one foot in front of the other, I find truth, beauty, and goodness, which I could sum up this way: God meets us in the most ordinary things, and through them, he drives back the shadows. There are places—real, tangible places—where the God of love meets us, if only for a moment. And when we're drowning in despair, we go to those places to connect with that love. We go there to attain love, and by attaining it, we push back the despair, even if just a little.

Amber: Eat the Crackers

Our three oldest boys were given to us in three stair-stepped years, like Irish triplets. When they were all under the age of five, and we loaded up the minivan for a road trip, it was like preparing to travel as a circus, complete with small dwelling places, swings, and pumping machinery. We were a spectacle. At gas stations, I carried one kid like a football, wore another one on my back, and kept track of the third by placing my pinky in his little hand. Across the south—Tennessee, Mississippi, Alabama, Louisiana—people blessed my heart, said things like, "Oh Lord, Mama. Three boys are a handful!" And they were right, but because we had close family across state borders, it was worth the insanity.

Back then, we still had Black Bayou. Seth's mom's side of the family still had that back wall of windows at Grandmom and Grandad's place, and we could watch the sun rise and set over the water from the long table. According to the time of day, we sat together with either coffee or gin watching anhingas and egrets. The picture windows showed a tree canopy that had been crafted over decades, spread tall and wide. The hostas arched out in artful layers against feathery grasses. We were married so young that my memories of us there are full of energy, even with all the kids. Seth was more handsome and I more beautiful than either of us realized, and we were still handling life with two grabby-happy hands, gobbling up what we could—food, wine, design, charm, a sense of place, welcome, each other. We did what it took to be among the family in that particular place because there were miracles among us there, transformations that changed our family trajectory, and still some in the works. We didn't want to miss a thing.

If we were together as a family at all, we were celebrating. I wasn't used to it at first, because I did not come from a celebrational people as much as I did a survivalist people. But Grandad began supper prayers by leading us in the Doxology, and we sang it in harmony and looked in each other's eyes, squeezing hands, before he bellowed, "Bless this food to thy use and us to thy service, and keep us ever mindful of the needs of others." (Grandad's big southern drawl rendered "thy" as "dy," and some family members still say it that way, forever and ever amen.) Then everyone laughed and filled plates and drank wine and poked fun at each other's politics and seemed to call all of it holy. I wasn't used to it. It made me uncomfortable, all this celebrating and feasting and irreverent joking, even though I loved it. My upbringing—particularly as it related to things of faith—was straight-faced, reasoned, and focused on rightness. The prayers before meals were no less holy. They were just quieter and truly grateful for the food. *Feast* was never a word we used.

At that table, the men were the ones who'd hunted for the meat we ate (something familiar to me), but in Louisiana, the men were also the ones who cooked it. It was not so much upscale as it was so delicious that you'd sell a kidney to have the chance to eat it. Here are some of the meals I recall: crawfish over angel hair pasta; duck gumbo; red beans and rice; steamed shrimp; smothered quail. With all of it, there was plenty of wine, plenty of gin, and decades of laughter.

Grandmom and Grandad's Louisiana table will always be my favorite table, carved walnut and long enough for their four kids to bring their kids who also brought theirs. It was the living table of a great-grandmother, and she set it with southern precision, in decadent layers of greenery and understated class. We transitioned into true adulthood as we listened to stories around that table. There was always a primary topic to discuss, everyone had their say if they could fit into the conversation, and every disagreement—and there was plenty of disagreement—was good-natured because we were family.

Going to visit my people was very different. We're a lot more country than Seth's family, who is a bit more country club. We centered life on the table in Alabama too, but I grew up more in a skillet cornbread kind of way, down long dirt roads around people who filled their cellars with preserved food instead of bottles of wine. My people are from hills and barn raisings and bottle-fed calves, and I have a great deal of pride in that. This accounts for my toughness, my humor, my closeness to the natural world, my ability to cut somebody who's up to no good, and my ability to survive on cheese and saltine crackers with a little dab of hot sauce. Seth's people are from boggy waters, Spanish moss, clinking glasses, and a right place to put a fork. Both had their share of secrets and shadows. Neither was better or worse than the other. They were just different (except in the realm of hot sauce), and when I became Seth's wife, I was fascinated by the spectrum of what it meant to be who we are as Seth and Amber Haines.

I took to his people easily, and they took to me. I had never been called a princess before Grandad, and though I tended to hate talk like that (because I want to be taken seriously, not fluffily), I believed him when he said it to me. I was loved, and I was a granddaughter there. And maybe even on some mornings with a cup of coffee looking out at the quiet waters, just for a soft little minute, I was a princess, albeit a smart princess in pants. That sense of place his grandparents created taught me good things about myself that I hadn't known before. They were true of me without going to Louisiana, but going there helped me see them and live them out.

Grandmom was already sick when I met Seth, but her decline was slow enough that we still had time to learn from her. Once she was gone, we still gathered and tried to set the table in her way, but it wasn't the same. Grandad still sang to great-grandbabies, rocking them in his chair, but the deep grief of losing his lover set in thick. When we lost him and the house sold, nothing could have prepared me for the realization that some tables are only for a season.

Since those young years of learning how to sense the bloom in a wine and how to cross the line just enough to get a good laugh out of a story, we've experienced our own table of shifting seasons. It has been loud and full, surrounded by purposeful blessing over gobs of spaghetti, layers of cake, the pull of monkey bread, the pucker of berry tarts, and, of course, multiple servings of soup or beans from giant pots. We have mastered the art of lining up fold-out tables and making them fancy with cloths and candles. Our years as Anglicans were years of the longest tables, encircled by musicians and singing. I don't know how many tears fell or how many prayers and goose bumps were raised at that table, how many meetings were held or how many decisions were made. Our table became a place of healing and of untold stories finally given voice. We are Seth and Amber Haines, people of a gathered table.

When we first joined the Anglicans, it was the idea of the communion table that drew me in. I came to believe that an ever-present God was particularly present at the communion table, since he is the host there. He wasn't literally *in* the bread, they said, but his mystical presence was conveyed *through* it, somehow. This is the reason I chose to follow the ordination path. I wanted to be as close as possible to that mystical presence, to that table. That table and what was served there became, to me, the whole thing, the entire reason we met together. I wanted to hold the Eucharist in my hand, my mouth, and my body, even if all I was holding was a metaphor, an idea.

But along the way, the focus shifted, and when the centrifugal force in our community spun so tightly around our leader instead of the communion table, I was catapulted out of orbit. As it turns out, the metaphor of the Eucharist can go only so far when it lives exclusively in the mind or the imagination, when it's not also lived out in the body.

I wanted to fix our congregation for a long time, but I couldn't metaphor my way out of our confusion. When despair set into my ministry, I wanted to be fixed, to be safe and fed, but I couldn't think of a single thing to heal me:

not the table where the priest offered communion to me; not the table of my friends who wanted to preserve the church at the cost of my story; not even my own table, a table where our church used to gather for meals and music and laughter.

Our identities are tied to what and who feeds us. We are, in fact, what we eat. So what happens when we don't have a safe table? What happens when we stop eating altogether?

The memory of my inability to see God's love is strangely vivid for someone who was so far under the river of grief that she was blind. I remember not seeing God's love, not tasting it at the eucharistic table. The table where I'd once found so much life was no longer safe, because what was supposed to be nourishing was overshadowed by something else. So there was no bread to hold, and in the absence of bread, I groped around for something to stop the hunger pangs.

Now, here's a hard thing to confess. I don't want to write this, but I understand reaching for a gun. I understand reaching for another lover, a bottle, anything. How do you stop hunger when there's no food that can satisfy you? How do you keep that hunger from driving you crazy?

There was a season after the fall-apart when nothing felt safe or sane. When I left the house, I shook violently. I became obsessively afraid that I would stop my car in the middle of any four-way stop and cause a crash from every direction. Driving through a stoplight has been one of the bravest things I've done in my life, and no one knew it. There were days I didn't get in the car unless I had to, because it took so much energy to act like I was okay in front of the boys and to make it back home alive.

It's hard to explain, but in those days, I could hold our children, remember exquisite meals, see the food in the re-frigerator, and reach over in the night and know Seth was beside me, but none of it felt safe. If the Eucharist table could be robbed of safety and meaning, why couldn't any of these other things? Finding God in all things is easier said than done when you're in the middle of despair. How do you move forward when even the good things, the gifts, feel like loss?

It was obvious a long time ago that Seth would eventually become Catholic, so when the Anglican way became more and more hollow, it wasn't a surprise when he signed up for the Rite of Christian Initiation of Adults, even though I was still in the Anglican ordination process. Roman Catholic was a thing I never wanted to be, though I had become a sympathizer by the time Seth dropped the news that he was crossing the Tiber—a phrase some use to describe Protestants who join Team Pope. When I was in seminary in a church history course under Dr. Brunner (the best Lutheran this side of Luther himself), I learned that the very earliest church took Jesus's words on the Eucharist way more literally than the Anglicans did. When he said, "This is my body," that's what the church thought he meant. When the first Christians met together, it wasn't so they could meditate on a lovely metaphor; it was so they could receive the grace of his presence in the bread, in real life. The early church considered the physical presence of Jesus to exist in the bread, and that's what made it the blessed Eucharist. They came together for the purpose of eating this bread, which then literally became part of their bodies. They didn't take the idea of Jesus into their hearts; they took his flesh into their flesh.

When I heard this, I looked at some of my classmates and said, "What are we going to do?" and they said, "Amber, the pope. We have to get over it because we can't be Catholic and have a pope." So I tried to get over it, but I sympathized with Seth and Team Pope.

I had grown up feeling sorry for the Catholics, the ones with idols in their church windows, but my college roommate's Catholic mother was apparently something different. She was full of a generous faith and told me about the abuse she endured as a child, how when she closed her eyes, a kind man sat with her in a place full of flowers. He was with her through it all, in a garden, giving her a safe place in her mind. When she got older and heard about Jesus, she said, "I already know him," and that's how she came to faith. She learned the name of the one who had already shown up for her in the dark. Her trust in his comfort and provision didn't convince me to trust him at the time, but it did leave an impression, a kind of holy envy inside me.

I felt that holy envy again when Seth started going to the Adoration Chapel at St. Joseph's Church, even though I was still trying to prop up my ministry. This was in the days before I left the Anglican Church, and it was in the earlier days of his sobriety journey. The Adoration Chapel was a place of deep clarity for Seth, where he came to know he belonged to a people, and he didn't have to go through anyone to gain access there. It was perpetual, open twenty-four hours a day, and Jesus was always there welcoming whoever went there for rest, Catholic or not. I sensed that Christ met Seth there in his frustration too, and he obviously gave him the patience to stand by me and wait for me, even as I planned to continue in an unhealthy ministry role.

When it came Seth's time for confirmation, he didn't do it. The local Catholic priest suggested he might wait and pray that our whole family would enter the church, which I thought was ludicrous advice. *That'll be the day.* I also thought, *Wouldn't that be nice to have peace, to not be jumping through hoops, to think I could just sit down for a minute? To think there could be a place that my story couldn't wreck? To think that I could just be with Jesus, no confusion, no manipulation, just Jesus?*

It was a beautiful thought, but then again, if the host looks like a cracker and smells like a cracker, it's probably not a Most High God in the flesh, no matter how much I wanted it to be. No matter how desperately I wanted to be in the flesh-and-blood room with him.

I cannot think of anything more common and casual than crackers, but somehow that made the experience all the more subversively alluring. Something about it reminded me of who I am, my dirt-road self, the grime in my minivan floorboards, my set-table self, the linens in our woven bread baskets. That God would present himself in the tangible, low-brow, everyday nature of the Eucharist was beginning to make sense to me. It made me want to go see, and besides, if I was reaching and grabbing nothing where I was, what did I have to lose? There was nothing for me to wreck there.

The thought of going to the Adoration Chapel, of sitting before a consecrated host, was so beautiful to me that I planned to secretly visit the place even if people thought I was ridiculous. I didn't even tell Seth I was going, maybe because I didn't want him to get his hopes up. If nothing else, it would be a quiet and unhurried place.

I walked into the intensely beige Adoration Chapel at St. Joseph's Church, where candles were flickering, the prayers of the people casting shadows on the wall. I landed on my knees in that chapel, and I didn't get back up. It started with my imagination, the thought that I was in the room with Jesus, but it became suddenly real. If he could meet me on the floor, then he could certainly be present as the communion host. It was like the Louisiana table—going there helped me see that I was a part of something bigger.

In the darkest moments, all I wanted was to commune with Jesus, and so I kept going back to the Adoration Chapel. The conversations I had there with God were hard ones. He asked me if I was going to stay with him. I said, "Where else do I have to go?" Even in the loneliness and weirdness, I found Christ there in the gift of the Eucharist, even if I wasn't ingesting it, and I knew I was in good company. Tolkien, Merton, Day, O'Connor—these writers knew symbols, but they found Christ in common bread. And O'Connor once said of the Eucharist, "Well, if it's a symbol, to hell with it."[4]

I've been going to the Adoration Chapel for over two years now, and I'm sure some of my friends think I'm bonkers. When they ask what it's like, I tell them. I go into that chapel, and surrounded by the smell of incense, I find a kneeler. Sometimes I ask why everything with my ordination happened. Sometimes I don't care. Sometimes I rattle on and on in prayer. Sometimes I listen to the quiet. Sometimes my prayers sound like cussing, and there've been times when I counted the ridges in my fingernails so I wouldn't have to think about anything at all. I've found such peace that I've fallen asleep. I have watched grown men in suits weeping. I have seen the tiniest elderly women with their arms opened as wide as they could reach. I have seen a string of children wallowing in the pew while their mother's nose touches the ground. I once heard a man say, "Why? Why is this happening?" I have heard lament and praise.

I still don't know how I feel about several aspects of Catholicism, and I know there are plenty of people who've been abused in its ranks, just as there've been so many abused across all of Christianity. There have been grody popes. There have been land grabs and the subjugation of people and the misuse of money and power. I do not dismiss those facts. I feel them like a gaping wound some days. All the more, I cling to Jesus in the Eucharist, just like all those saints who've called power to account, who've tended to the poor, who've received the Eucharist (not taken it) as a source of strength and poured out their lives for the sake of others. Whether it's a metaphor or literal or both, the Eucharist empowers an embodied people to stand against injustice, even when all other power has been taken from them.

———

When I decided to leave the Anglicans and join the Catholics, I spoke with the priest at our new church home, told him that I had followed Jesus for a long time. I was ready to eat, I said, and it physically hurt not to receive the Eucharist, especially after being hungry for so long. "It's supposed to hurt," he said, and though I didn't understand exactly why the point was pain, I know now. There was transformation for me in that pain, and I was being asked to sit with Jesus in it. Sitting with Jesus is good even if it hurts.

As I practiced sitting in that pain week after week, I realized that there'd be no more reaching or flailing my arms or asking people to hear me or help me, not in this season. There'd just be me and the wounded Healer, and he'd help me find my way to a new table if I fixed my eyes on the Divine Love in adoration. I never expected to find such a table there, such a feast in the midst of heartache.

For me, it was as simple as a cracker. Whatever there is to sort out about the Eucharist, I hope you do it. I hope it frustrates you. I hope there's an end to the metaphors for us all. Let it be real. Let it go to our stomachs and our heads and become the muscle that moves us. The grace of the table is that it feeds an eternal hunger. What else will do?

Practice: Receive Communion

Maybe the idea of Christ becoming present in bread and wine is a stretch for you. Maybe you see Jesus's teaching in John 6:54—"Those who eat my flesh and drink my blood have eternal life, and I will raise them up on the last day" (NRSV)—as a metaphor. Wherever you are with the theological nuances of communion, the bedrock reality is that God works through the stuff of earth to bring us into the awareness of his presence.

Find a time and place to receive communion, the Eucharist, the Lord's Supper, whatever you call it. When you do, imagine that you are there not to take but to receive. Read these words of Christ at the Last Supper and imagine yourself there with him and the disciples:

> While they were eating, Jesus took bread, and when he had given thanks, he broke it and gave it to his disciples, saying, "Take and eat; this is my body."
>
> Then he took a cup, and when he had given thanks, he gave it to them, saying, "Drink from it, all of you. This is my blood of the covenant, which is poured out for many for the forgiveness of sins. I tell you, I will not drink from this fruit of the vine from now on until that day when I drink it new with you in my Father's kingdom." (Matt. 26:26–29)

Imagine further: What if Jesus comes to be tangible to you? What if he wants you to touch, taste, and smell him? What if he wants you to be a tangible representation of him? Make this part of your communion meditation.

If you're not in a place where communion is readily available, consider the practice of spiritual communion. Sit in a quiet place and imagine the bread and wine, the body and blood in front of you. Imagine taking, eating, and drinking. Ask to experience God in that silent moment of imagination.

four

CREATE SIGNS

Seth: Cairnal People

I like to imagine the moment the earth was pushed up from the sea. Tectonic plates smashed together, and the earth buckled, pushing rock heavenward. The Himalayas, the Rockies, and the Alps rose from their sleeping sea beds to look down on the world. Their little sister, the Ozark Mountains, did too, and those big brothers looked down with awe, because down her slim spine, God ran a seam of silver—the Buffalo River.

In the Ozarks, the early spring rains soak the hardwoods before falling onto moss-covered limestone. Drops roll down the faces of those rocks and soak the forest floor. What's not caught in the roots of the ferns, dogwoods, and redbuds trickles to the edges of those mountains, collects in tiny streams that sometimes follow the hiking trails, sometimes pour off hundred-foot cliffs. Always, though, the runoff makes its way down to the river bottom, sliding over and under the rocks that, as Norman MacLean put it, were pulled "from the basement of time."[1]

The early days of spring bring color to the mountains. There is a shade of new green so full of life that you can almost feel it humming in your chest. The river takes that emerald color too, and the white, pink, and purple flowering trees hang over those waters like a wreath on a bride's head. It's the idyllic place for a wedding, and on a spring day in 2017, I watched as a bride and groom made their vows on the banks. After the pronouncement, the kiss, and the introduction of the couple, she took his hand and led him straight into the river, wedding dress and all. They rollicked in the water like children, and I supposed it was a sort of baptism of their union. Two sacraments at once, all under the gaze of the limestone giants rising up over the water.

The spring waters don't attract just the occasional bride. They also bring kayakers, canoers—the folks my friend Colin calls "the paddlers," of which he is one. The paddlers make their way down the high water, raise a beer to the two sleepy boulders in the pool at Steele Creek. Sometimes they shore their tiny boats and play in the falls just to the northeast. Once, I saw a group of six strip naked and shower under those falls. I was smallmouth hunting within easy eyeshot, knee deep in the water and working an angle with my fly rod just upstream. They didn't seem to care.

The spring brings through-hikers and locals down to the water's edge too. They are people marked by adventure, and their backpacks, bumper stickers, and tattoos say as much. They're devotees of Patagonia—the gear, not the place—and on more than one occasion, I've noticed Tolkien's quote splashed on the bumper sticker of an old pickup in the Steele Creek parking area: "Not all those who wander are lost."[2] In the first summer of the pandemic, I met Andy on those banks, a writer with a sort of nerd-fusion tattoo of Finn and Jake (from *Adventure Time*) dressed, respectively, as Han

Solo and Chewbacca (from *Star Wars*). To date, it's the only tattoo that's inspired jealousy.

The newlyweds, paddlers, naked bathers, and through-hikers love their symbols, their reminders of adventure. And none of those symbols—whether brand logos, slogans, or tattoos—speak to me quite like the cairns in the valley. Along the banks, the river's parishioners stack smooth stones to create towers. Sometimes those towers are small and delicate, almost swaying with any wind. Some of these cairns, though, seem built to last a lifetime. They are sturdy, raised on a base of several large rocks and tapering to a final tiny rock three or more feet off the ground. I've stumbled across cairn yards on those shores, places holding dozens of those memorials. Memorials to what? To the journey, to the people who've gone before us, to the people who will come behind us? I can't say.

Humans seem to be cairn creatures, which is to say people who crave and create icons, memorials, monuments, and altars. We've been this way from the beginning of time, which is why we don't find cairns just on the banks of the Buffalo. They dot the Appalachian Trail, the Scottish Highlands, the Middle East, Africa, and Mongolia.

In the Scriptures, we read of the cairnal drive of the faith fathers. Jacob erected a cairn after his bizarre ladder dream in which God promised to multiply his descendants. He set up another on the location where God changed his name from Jacob to Israel. Joshua dragged twelve stones from the riverbed and set them up in the promised land. Samuel set up a stone named Ebenezer after God defeated the Israelites' mortal enemies, the Philistines. Elijah stacked rocks in his great showdown with the prophets of Baal.

The early Christians had their own stone memorials in the catacombs, and they stacked stones to create churches. Church artists chiseled sculptures from stones, sculptures of David, Moses, Mary, and Jesus. They didn't stop with stones, though. They made icons, images of Christ and the saints that reminded them of the stories of redemption, healing, and resurrection. Like us, like all humankind, they were a cairnal, memorializing, iconographic people, and they stacked, chiseled, and painted as if to say, "Take a moment to remember."

As a child, I knew little of altars, memorials, and icons. In the Baptist church I attended with my mother and sister, we had a table at the front of the sanctuary that read, "Do this in remembrance of me." It was not a cairn, per se, but it was a sort of altar meant to remind us that everything we did was in contemplation of Christ's grand act of love. That message was most pronounced when, once every quarter, that table held trays of tiny, saltless crackers and grape-juice shots. The table became our cairn, our place of remembering the life, death, and resurrection of Christ.

When I was a Baptist child in a Catholic school, the volume of icons, statues, and altars was overwhelming. Mary, Joseph, Jesus, some saints—their likenesses were set around the school and church. When I passed through the doors at Immaculate Conception Elementary School, I was greeted by a statue of the mother of God, and when I was excused to use the restroom, I passed by Jesus and his sacred heart. Memorials were everywhere, always looking down on me, and if I would have listened, I might have heard them echo the words of St. Stephen just before his stoning at the hands of the religious leaders: "Look up, look up, look up."

My Grandma Ducky—called this on account of the ducks that frequented the bayou in her backyard—was a proper Episcopalian, and she'd been through a life season of extravagant drunkenness. By her own admission and the admission of my mother, she was a shoe-throwing drunk, a deadeye and a woman with a short fuse. But when she finally dried out in the hospital, when she met Christ—the Divine Love who reordered her life—she changed. This is not to say my

61

grandmother was bereft of fire in sobriety. She still ran a little hot and was prone to combine curses with prayer. (Her favorite expression for any screwup was "Dammit! 'Scuse me, Lord.") Still, in sobriety Grandma Ducky was more at peace with herself and the world, and she memorialized that peace with her own house altars, although she wouldn't have called them that.

I remember her little tributes to St. Francis the best. There was a smallish St. Francis in the desk where she kept her Bible, a journal, and a black book of phone numbers. There was one in the backyard near the birdbath and fountain. There were others, I know, though my memory has lost track of where they hid. She had a penchant for Francis, she said, because he reminded her to be a channel of peace, which is to say Francis reminded her to look up to the source of her peace, most especially when she grew thirsty.

Years after she made her way to eternal peace, I took a page from her book. When the Divine Love led me out of the fog of drunkenness and into sobriety, I remembered my grandmother's story, her journey, her love of St. Francis. Knowing I needed my own icon of channeled peace, I made my way to the tattoo artist and had him ink an interpretation of a thirteenth-century fresco on my left inner arm. The tattoo was a recasting of Giotto's portrayal of St. Francis preaching to the birds. He is with me every day, and in those moments when he catches my eye, he reminds me that God can be found in even the humblest things, things like birds and sobriety.

Memorials—whether cairns, icons, or statues—are meant to be places of remembrance. They can be elaborate, like the stone statues of Mary in my Catholic school days or the ink of St. Francis on my left arm. They can be simple, like the wooden table at the front of my Baptist church. They can be tiny, like the cairns on the riverbed. But always, they point us to the timeless, transcendent numinosity operating in the world.

Over the last two years, Amber has created tiny memorials in our home. They remind us of the deep magic God spoke into the world. They remind Amber of hope.

At Southern Mercantile in Prairie Grove, she turned a corner and discovered a little Madonna dressed in blue and the arched, rose-dotted pedestal that held her. She brought it to me, told me she had to have it—it was not a request—and that was that. There she found another icon, a triptych showing Mary holding the baby Jesus, St. Francis looking on from the right panel, the apostle John looking on from the left. The mother of Jesus, Jesus's best friend, the saint who'd bear the stigmata years later—all called to suffering, all accepting it willingly because of their strong hope in the promise of eternal love. She set those icons together in the entryway, just above a small bookshelf, and when I see this sort of altar, when I toss my keys onto it after a long day of work, I'm reminded of a deeper and more transcendent magic.

Across from that altar, on the other side of the room, Amber hung a triad of icons over an old New England side table. There's the modern Mary Magdalene with her bandanna and nose ring, an icon from the artist Gracie Morbitzer. There are the more traditional icons, one of the myrrh-bearing women and the other of Mary Magdalene and the mother of Jesus bowing at Christ's theophany—that moment when the dove descended and Jesus was revealed as the Son of God. Why did Amber choose these icons, even before the dark days set in? What did they say to her? What do they say to her now?

Across the room and over the fireplace, a golden Madonna hides behind a viny plant. This golden Madonna is her favorite because "she seems strong, but she's actually delicate."

Standing in the middle of the room, you cannot escape the gaze of these saints. They are icons of calling and suffering. They are icons of hope too. And taken together, they form three separate memorials. They are places to remember the journeys of Francis, John, the women, Mary Magdalene, and Christ's mother. Three separate reminders of those called to glory through sorrow. Three separate reminders to ask for the help of the Divine Love who rescued each.

Not unlike the stacked stones on the riverbank, these images that line our walls are icons of hope. They remind us of those who suffered their own seasons of despair but somehow managed to find their way through them. If we bend our ears toward them, we can hear them say, "Look up to the hills—where will your help come from?"

I have spent years on the banks of the Buffalo River and over two decades on her twin sister, the White River. All those years, all those cairns, and never once have I seen a band of coyotes stacking stones or hanging triptychs on trees. I've not witnessed the oddity of an elk painting Mary, clothed in blue. There have been no white-tailed deer with St. Francis tattoos or bumper stickers on their hindquarters proclaiming, "Not all those who wander are lost." Memorial making is a human eccentricity, I think, something baked into our DNA, and I wonder: Why? Perhaps it's nothing more than sentimentality, a way of making more out of a moment than it really is. Or maybe it's because we are the descendants of Adam and Eve, people who set up markers that point us in the direction of home. Perhaps these cairns, these memorials remind us that even as we navigate this valley of deathly shadows, there is a way through, if only we keep our eyes on the markers.

Amber: Memorials Everywhere in Everyone

Twenty years ago, the second summer after we were married, Seth took a six-week clerkship at a Little Rock law firm while I studied poetry in Ireland. We were apart for eight weeks, which is a thing I can't fathom now. I was twenty-two and still wanted to see the world, mostly the world of my ancestors, who were said to be some glorious mix of Scotch-Irish royalty and cattle thieves. I wanted to know where my people came from and expected that sense of place to help me better understand my own story, who I am, and what I'm made of. So after Ireland, my friend Brooke and I spent a week hopping the train and staying in hostels across Scotland, the land of my maiden name.

We made it through Glasgow to Oban, arriving at the end of the day, and a stranger told us to go stand by the water. "You'll never see a sunset like Oban's anywhere else in the world." I haven't seen one like it since. We waited there until a box of melted crayons was pulled across the round sky. Brooke and I weren't yet mothers. We were wearing hiker backpacks with pillows strapped to the side, balancing on our skinny young legs at the edge of our small world.

We traveled from there to Kyle of Lochalsh and the Isle of Skye. We saw castle walls jutted above the fog caped low on the hills. There were nods to the Loch Ness monster up toward Inverness and entire fields of lavender on the way to Edinburgh. There were rock walls, thatched roofs, and fireplaces burning peat, and there were cairns everywhere. Some of them were burial sites. Some of them marked grounds for worship thousands of years ago. They were there to point to what is beyond the here and now, but the locals also taught me that cairns are meant to give travelers direction. Most of the time, a cairn says, "Don't go that way; come this direction." It is a road sign that can't be washed away or stolen without a great deal of effort. A cairn tells the traveler, "You're right where you're supposed to be. Keep going."

That summer, I stood in the pubs, a young wife a long way from home. I drank pints and listened like a witness to the sounds that gave birth to Appalachian music. I laughed with strangers. I missed home, but I didn't threaten to return before my time. Instead, I felt magic in the shape of wave-hewn rocks along the shores. I felt a deep sense of home in both Ireland and Scotland. Instead of rushing back, I stayed weeks longer, crossed borders, counted money with different faces, ate hearty stews, and studied homesickness and what it means to feel at home so far away.

I was there to study poetry, which is the study of sacramentality at its finest, though I wouldn't have known that at the time. I've since learned that a book of Wallace Stevens's poetry is titled *A Poet Looks at the World the Way a Man Looks at a Woman*. This is an example of what I found when trying to give a succinct definition of what it means to study poetry, but almost every good definition is a quote from a poet. It's as if poetry is required to explain poetry.

Poetry captures a deeper understanding of the world, revealing something hidden or what often goes uncaptured. Poetry is human, and according to researchers, robots can't write it, at least not well.[3] Coming from the Greek word *poiēsis*, which means "to create," poetry acts more like a verb, a way to engage the world with treasure-hunter eyes—most particularly the discovery of emotion or meaning through written image and sound.

When I let my feet feel the rock shorelines, I was studying poetry. When I tromped through tall stinging nettle, being stung all over my summer-exposed skin to get a closer look at a fifth-century monastery, I was studying poetry. When I contemplated jumping in the raging sea because of the nettles but felt even more drawn to see the stacked stones, I was studying poetry.

Ireland and Scotland changed the way I look at the world, which may eventually have saved our marriage when nothing felt right about it anymore. My own undealt-with past had remained very present, while the law kept Seth from being present at all. In that season, we would visit his grandparents, who were emblems (memorials and icons) of staying and repairing. They were magic, embodiers of poetry and embodiers of hope, and I saw them as a sign for the direction I wanted to go. You could call them living cairns. So I stayed, and we worked to repair. We took the long way, but we're stronger now for having kept going, for having seen the cairns along the way.

Like stacked stones in Scotland, memorials surround us every day if we train our eyes to see them. Maybe we tend to recognize them a little easier when we feel lost, when we know we need a sign. These sacramental objects or people or places are like little arrows pointing *beyond* this present moment and also very specifically *to* this present moment. When we recognize a person or a thing or a place that helps us see beyond the moment into who we are and who God is, or what it means to love and be loved, that's a sacramental thing. That's a grace.

When we look at the stacked stones of a cairn or when our eyes catch the light from a golden-hued icon, we see a convergence of past, present, and future. Someone who's been there before (from the past) tells us where we're supposed to be (in the present) and invites us to keep going (into the future). A cairn recognizes part of our story, where we've been. It says, "Look, you've made it this far, and yes, there's more to the journey." This is what it means to have sacramental eyes, to see all the parts of the story as avenues of grace. Even if in the moment we feel lost or like we're drowning, a story can reach out to us and remind us we're still on the journey toward the fullness of love, which is the fullness of God's presence, which is where we're known, transformed, healed, and most fully ourselves. We can get up and keep going. There's grace to receive from yesterday, and that grace sends us out into the future in hope.

———

It's true that all the Marys in this house are beautiful. I didn't mean to collect them. I've just been drawn to them. I'd have to be paralyzed to be as meek as any one of those little Mary renditions, so it's funny. It's taken all these images for me to even begin a small devotion to her, and I still have a hard time feeling mothered by her. My trinitarian theology shies me away from her even as I say my Hail Marys—the Catholic prayers asking for Mary's intercession—and I do say them, because the rosary is a practice of landing still with my palms up, and those beads—those little rocks between my fingers—are cairnal reminders.

Mary invites a release in me when my habit is nothing short of a stranglehold on everything I love. When I least expect it, Mary's image evokes a story that I understand more than anything else about myself, the one of mother love, the one of watching a son suffer and not being able to help him. Her image evokes worship, but not toward her. She only, always, and ever points toward the love of a God who writes a story more beautifully than I could ever write for someone I love. Mary points to the ultimate God of the verb *poiēsis*. Her story is one of yes and of release. When I experience pain over, for, and with a son, it's Mary who says to me, "I know it's hard. I believe you. Palms up. Keep going."

It seems to me that the memorials with the most effect are the ones with relatable stories attached to them, and at the end of the day, everything has a story. More often than not, those stories acknowledge something of our pain, our journey, our incurable humanity. That's why the most relatable memorials say, "I believe you," which are some of the most powerful words I've ever heard. They tell us we're seen and heard and were expected to show up in this place. They tell us there's a path of healing for us. Memorials can be the exit ramp from trauma loops and obsessive thinking, a way to move forward again.

In the days after my ministry cratered and my sense of place, identity, and vocation was gutted, the stories of women who have come through despair called me out of those deepest waters of grief, at least enough to get a breath. The image of Mary all over the house whispered to me again and again that my passion and my sense of self and of God would return to me. She is the mother of Christ, and we are Christ's adopted siblings, so, in a sense, don't we belong to her? And if we follow Christ, just as she did, won't each of us have a sorrow to bear? She knows.

Mary Magdalene, too, spoke to me: "I know. I believe you. Your voice matters even when they don't listen. Keep telling what you've seen. Keep bearing witness to the truth."

Hildegard—the twelfth-century German abbess, writer, naturalist, artist, mystic, and saint—sits in our kitchen window, holding a little pot of flowers. When I spend hours working the garden and I begin hurting all over, she reminds me, "It all works together." She says, "But if you don't write, even when you feel a little crazy, you'll land sick in bed." Because she herself landed sick in bed from not writing, I'm learning to not let myself be away from the deeper, written soul-work for long.

These women who have gone before me are road signs reminding me of who I am and where I'm headed. They remind me there's a story going on here, and it's not over. They remind me there are very real women in my very real life who live similar stories, even though none of them would be quick to claim sainthood. The Goshen Girls are some of those women.

We already knew Ashlyn Gagnon and her husband, Jesse, from our Anglican Church days, and we long imagined living near them and the brewery they were opening on their homeplace (Orthodox Farmhouse Brewery). We'd bought land near them in the land of Goshen (Arkansas, that is), and in the fall of 2022, we broke ground on what will be our permanent home. From that little outpost, we intend to trade sugar, share tools, and help tend to the Gagnons' chickens when they're out of town. We'll watch their kids if they ever need it, buy pints to support their brewery, send our boys to help them build or mend fences. I'm sure we'll share dinners and stories and maybe a song or two over the years. This is all to say that the Gagnons are the kind of people we hope to live life with for a long time, especially after what we've endured together in the church.

When people meet Ashlyn, they tend to stick around. She has a way about her that's hard to pin down. Maybe it's her ability to woo coupled with her cooking skills. Maybe it's her giant smile and her ability to make people feel at home no matter where they're from. When a local beef farmer named Emily reached out to Jesse to ask about grains from the brewing process, Ashlyn quickly took up with Emily. As we've come to know Emily, Ashlyn and I have started calling her "the salt of the earth." Want an icon? See Emily. In sunlight, her hair catches fire, and her eyes are seawater blue-green. She's quiet and funny, and she is strong. At thirty weeks pregnant, she was easily outworking every human I'd ever met. We happened to have bought our land from her dad, who had already told me about her and her big sister, Liz, who lived nearby. Liz is a single mom with a corporate career. She's also a sheep farmer and has always dreamed of starting a farmers market in Goshen to connect local food with local people. She's the biggest dreamer I've met and sees a world without food insecurity as a doable thing.

It was easy for Ashlyn and me to take our cues from Liz. We'd discussed wanting to see a farmers market get off the ground too. Our little beloved town of Goshen is one you can blink and miss if you're just on your way to the Buffalo River, but for those of us who have lived there, we know the potential. We know the houses by what we see each other growing. When I met Emily and Liz's dad, he was talking about their mama, Ms. Mary, who is a master gardener and preserver. I said, "Oh! Ms. Mary is the one who grows all those amazing peonies!"

We planned our first meeting to discuss the potential for a farmers market and met in Liz's house surrounded by a hundred house plants, which is how I knew I loved her. We left having decided we could and should and would make the market happen. When we had our first official meeting as the board of directors, Brett came too, a gorgeous soul from the Northeast with experience running a nonprofit and with every ounce of get-up-and-go as the rest of us. Maybe more. She happens to live right up the road, growing sunflowers and cooking gluten-free dishes as much a feast for the eyes as for the mouth.

Now every Thursday evening until sunset, we set up market booths for Goshen's makers and local growers. We usually have musicians playing and a food truck. In the throes of the pandemic, there were evenings when the virus never crossed my mind, because we were outside with plenty of room, kids darting across the lawn. The Arbor Board walks through pointing to their monarch butterflies. Everyone is proud. A few nights of the year, our sponsors provide free food for the entire town, and so many folks come to eat that we always run out. My boys set up the picnic tables for the guests, and people will come and sit with us, listening to the music until we take the tents down.

It's easy to spend every spare second looking at a screen, at the filtered faces on Instagram with ten-step plans for a more click-worthy life, but it seems harder online to stop and look for cairns and memorials, much less make them. It's easy to find them in the little altars, statues, and icons around my house. It's even easier to recognize them among our local farmers and the people who want to support them. It's hard to miss the icons, the magic, and the poetry when you're close to the earth, when you're in a field of hay helping load watermelons into an old lady's trunk. It has been hard for me to not see the Divine Love as I have come to know my neighbors' names, when one gives my oldest son a bag of quail feathers so he can tie beautiful flies that allow him to catch more rainbow trout.

The market is a memorial to me, something that reminds me not just who God is but also who I am. I was made to be an organizer and planner, a starter and dreamer, a grower and connector. I was made to appreciate what it takes to feed a people with nourishing food, which reminds me of what my previous role as curate was supposed to be. Every Thursday is a reminder that my work is sacred. It's a sort of cairn that reminds me that where I've been, where I am, and where I'm going is sacred.

When we make memorials or come across any icon, cairn, or sacramental thing of creation, we name it as sacred, allow it to point to something that is beyond us. There we see a timeless, transcendent, deeper magic—the magic of the Divine Love operating in the world—and it reminds us who we are. There, in that reminder, we feel ourselves becoming a sign.

Practice: Build a Cairn

In 2019, our family visited the White River for a bit of a fall break. It was a good trip, one in which we ate pumpkin dump cake (if you know, you know), watched *Adventure Time*, played card games, and fished for rainbow trout. It was a memorable trip, and at the end, we stopped by a particularly rocky portion of the river, grabbed smooth stones, and took them home to turn into memorials with white paint markers. We'd discussed goals on that trip, and each of us wrote a goal on a rock as a sort of memorial. Amber wrote, "Find our land" on her rock, and she did later that year.

We're not suggesting you write your goals on a rock. We are suggesting, however, that you find a stone, a piece of concrete, a brick, or something that will outlast you and write on it something (or someone) bringing you hope these days. Put the memorial somewhere you'll see it regularly. When you experience some new thing bringing you hope, add it to the stone. In this way, you'll begin to build a sort of cairn of remembrance, a cairn of hope.

If writing on rocks is a bit too on the nose for you, get an old mason jar and some smallish slips of paper. When some moment of hope-bearing truth, beauty, or goodness happens, record it on one of those slips and put it in the jar. Keep the jar in a conspicuous place as a kind of memorial.

five

PRACTICE SILENCE

Seth: Flee the World

The soybean fields of the Arkansas River valley are an ocean. There are places where the green rows swell from the dirt and carry on for miles, each row spaced with impossible symmetry like the morning swells that roll in from the Gulf of Mexico. Broad leaves ripple in the wind and dance in the rain, and their movement produces a sort of low whisper. Cowbirds and red-winged blackbirds flit from these soybean fields to the barbed wire fences of neighboring pastures. For all my time spent in the fields, I do not remember whether these birds made a noise, but even if they did, would I have heard it over the loud odor of rich dirt, the sweet smell of cow dung and natural gas?

When I was seventeen, I worked the nastiest job of my life in those fields. I'd been hired by a natural gas production company that worked the valley, and on my first day of the job, the foreman gave me my summer assignment. The well-heads leaked, he said, and there were plenty of government regulations against allowing those leaks to go untreated. So in order to keep off the government's bad list, they hired me to do the dirty work—bioremediation, he called it.

I made my way into the fields in the company's old Chevy with a busted radio and barely blowing air conditioner. I took dusty river roads, found the leased sections that housed the leaky wellheads, and got to work. My job was an act of faith. I grabbed the industrial plastic bag from the truck bed. It was filled with a fine grayish powder, and if I was to believe the biologist who'd explained the matter, that powder was full of dormant microorganisms that came to life upon contact with any moisture—rainwater, natural gas runoff, urine. So day after day, I visited the wellheads, sprinkled that chalk dust over natural spills, and tilled it under. On most days, the soil was so wet that I spent hours standing shin deep in a bio-petrol slurry. In that slurry, the bugs broke their hibernation and feasted on the petroleum in ravenous silence.

It would take six months for those microorganisms to have any remedial effect, the biologist said. Six months, and the noisy messes of men dissipated under the persistent, monastic silence of an invisible bug. I'm sure his claims are quantifiable, and I suppose there are biologists who could explain the science of it all, but at seventeen, I'm not sure I cared. I was not paid to understand the science. I was paid to be a grunt.

I do not remember the songs of that summer on account of the fact that I spent eight hours a day either in a radioless truck or in a radioless soybean field. Once, I brought an old cassette Walkman along so I could listen to The Police's *Synchronicity* on repeat. I ruined the Walkman and the accompanying tape when I dropped them in the slurry, and that was the end of that. I don't really remember too many conversations from that summer either, though the biologist traveled with me from time to time and tried to impart life lessons, which I mostly ignored because I was a teenager. I'm sure I filled the valley with the noise of the tiller, but I don't really remember that either. When I think about the summer of 1995, I think mostly about the silence.

Working the soybean fields with no music, no companionship, and no cell phone was about the closest thing I experienced to being on a deserted island. I went entire days without speaking a single word, not even to the farmers who'd sometimes drive by on their tractors. I got acquainted with birds and worms and the occasional king snake. Sometimes I'd moo out the window at a cow herd, not because I thought it ironic or funny but because talking with a cow is better than talking with nothing at all. (I understand how Tom Hanks's character formed such a meaningful relationship with a volleyball in *Cast Away*.)

I don't regret my summer of bioremediation. It was nasty, physical labor, and it ruined at least a couple of pairs of boots and a Walkman. But it was honest and quiet work, and sometimes I think this is where I first recognized the wonder of silence. In those fields, there were no right or wrong answers. There was no one to please either, except the biologist who'd entrusted me with a menial task. There were no intrusions into my interior life, except for the occasional roughneck or two who happened to stop by a wellhead while I was working, but they mostly just grunted their hellos, offered me a smoke, then went on their way. There was plenty of space to think, organize my thoughts, ruminate about the future. It was space I wasn't afforded in my other circles, particularly faith circles.

Like many evangelicals, I was raised to believe that great faith is characterized by great noise. Our congregation had a humdinger of a pipe organ and a brass section that was both large and mostly in tune. Our preacher was pretty laidback, but there was a moment in every Sunday service when both his ire and his volume reached for the rafters. Our youth services were real bangers too—loud games, loud bands, loud jokes—and everything was "amped" or "next level" or "peak." I cannot remember a single moment of actual silence. During our altar call moments, Jesus softly and tenderly called through the low drone of that humdinger pipe organ.

I understand the application of noise to any space of silence, even religious silence. Silence, after all, conjures one of two primary emotional states—absolute boredom or abject terror. What teenager wants to sit in Quakeresque silence waiting for the Spirit to move and shake a word free from Sister Letha when he could be chatting up Sister Letha's daughter at the coffee shop? What adult wants to sit in that same silence and wonder whether the money will outstrip the month's obligations, whether the chemotherapy will take hold, whether the wayward son will ever return? Put another way, silence doesn't always feel good. But if I had learned the lessons from that summer of silence, I might have understood how important it is to clear the decks. And, as I'd find eighteen years later, clearing the decks makes space for God.

Three decades, a marriage, and four children into living, I woke from a heavy season of drinking into sobriety. In the waking, without booze to silence the existential narratives of pain, everything felt so noisy. Voices were so loud that I couldn't hear anything, especially not the still, small voice of God. So I set out to organize those voices and clear the decks. And I set out to do it in silence. How? I wrote of the practice in *The Book of Waking Up*:

> In the days of my darkest pain, I sat in my living room chair every night and asked the God of comfort to come sit with me in my pain. In that chair, I contemplated the narratives of scarcity, how I hadn't had enough faith to be cured of asthma or to see my son cured. I considered the seeming

absence of God. I shared my pain in prayer with the God I
questioned, and made meditative space for him to work (or
not). In the stillness and silence of that space, releasing all
expectations, here's what I found: the Healer of healers, the
Great Physician began to soften the sting in his Divine Love.[1]

In the silence, away from the noise of the world, the noise
of my mind met its match. In the silence, the Divine Love
came and brought peace to all things, even the unanswered
questions.

Now, here's the dumbfounding thing about it: even after
experiencing the power of interior silence, I forgot that power.
When I entered my forty-first year, and we were months away
from our Anglican escape, my inner life became so noisy
again. Amber was falling deeper into the river of grief, and
I did my best to shoulder it. I had my own noisy thoughts
too, my own grief and anger to navigate. In the hours after
midnight, the inner voices screamed at me, demanded that
I wake up and listen. They recounted two years of wrongs,
slights, ways in which a sacramental community of peace had
spun into chaos. Those voices reminded me of the lines the
priest had crossed in his conversations with Amber—how
men and women working together should deal with their
attractions for each other, how they shouldn't be afraid of
erotic love. I flogged myself for not confronting him sooner,
thinking Amber's ordination would somehow level the playing field and smooth out the turmoil. Another voice came
haunting from time to time, one that imagined all the harm
I might do if left alone in a room with him. Sometimes I still
hear that voice.

In those months, the inner noise was deafening. The cloister of my own mind was no cloister at all. It was a subway
station, a place where many thoughts arrived and departed.
There were crowds in my head, a mob, and I needed them

silenced. So I did what I'd learned to do in the early days of sobriety. I returned to silence.

On Monday mornings, I snuck out of the house at 5:45 a.m. and made my way to the Adoration Chapel a few miles from home. There I gathered with a small group of regulars whose faces I'd come to know. We did not speak but instead entered into silence, faces turned toward the sacrament at the altar. I sat alone in a pew, sometimes knelt in prayer. I turned to the Gospels in the silence, read of the Christ who cast out demons and healed the deaf and silenced the noise of men. I read of the Christ who himself pursued silence with the God of the universe. There I confessed my anger, my inner chaos, asked Christ to wake up and still the storm that made so much noise in my inner ear. And over time— months in fact—the mob retreated. The crowd dispersed.

In *The Power of Silence*, Cardinal Robert Sarah writes of the human need to flee from the noisy world and connect with God. This need is memorialized in the monastic tradition through the Latin term *fuga mundi*, which means "flight from the world." Of *fuga mundi*, he writes, "It means an end of the turmoil, the artificial lights, the sad drugs of noise and the hankering to possess more and more goods, so as to look at heaven. A man who enters the monastery seeks silence in order to find God. He wants to love God above all else, as his sole good and his only wealth."[2]

Monasteries are for silence, for finding God and ultimately for discovering love that silences internal turmoil. I've learned this from books but also from life. I learned it in the soybean fields in the river valley, in my evening silence in the early days of sobriety, and in the tiny Adoration Chapel in Fayetteville, Arkansas. I learned to love silence through practice.

I think a lot about Cardinal Sarah's comments, about how my natural inclination is to pursue turmoil, the artificial, the drugs of noise and consumption. I consider my penchant for booze to silence the noise of pain or the roiling of my brain over the slights of a spiritual leader. But I also think about the ways I'll fill any silent moment with activity, with scrolling a social media feed or watching a video on YouTube or reading reviews for the perfect replacement backpack. (I am a bit of a bag junkie.) I consider how I fill even my workspaces with background noise. In all this noise, is there room to hear the voice of hope? Is there space to catch the whisper of the Divine Love?

In his book *Silence: In the Age of Noise*, Dutch explorer Erling Kagge writes, "The starry sky 'is the truest friend in life, when you've first become acquainted; it is ever there, it gives ever peace, ever reminds you that your restlessness, your doubt, your pains are passing trivialities.'"[3] I have found this to be true in my life, but the point is not the "starry sky"; the point is the silence. In the silence of my evening chair or the hour of cloister in the chapel, I have come to understand that every pain is passing, every wound can be healed. In the silence, I have heard the voice of the God who whispers: hope.

Amber: Unresisting the Quiet

I close the bedroom door behind me. Seth's in the kitchen cooking dinner again. I can smell the mirepoix and the filé, two of my favorite smells on the planet. It's Cajun night, and he's got Louisiana in his blood, which means he's good at cooking like the other men in his family. It is possible that in our twenty-three years of marriage, his cooking has saved his life a few times or, at minimum, our marriage. He's been cooking most of our suppers for a few years now, which makes even more sense when you consider that beyond biscuits and cornbread, cooking is as unnatural to me as silence is. I'm liable to overcook everything I touch (overdoer that I am), and it is my least favorite thing to work hard at something and still be garbage at it.

Before Seth's good cooking became the evening norm, he quit his job as an attorney to start a business as a writer, and I was thrilled we'd get that kind of time together. I imagined him at his desk and me at a desk in the other room. We'd both be clicking away and doing what we love, writing books, having lunch and afternoon delight. Yet, it seemed the more he accomplished, the less I got done. The more he wrote, the fewer words came out of me. I couldn't figure it out. But then we had what I call the String Light Incident.

We lived in Goshen then, up that dirt road, and had a porch that stretched across the back of the entire house overlooking the wooded hills. I worked hard to string lights in a zigzag design above the porch, but then a storm blew them down and shattered thin glass in every direction, into the chairs, down the stairs, and everywhere there was to walk.

Before the string lights broke, Seth had been going outside to work so he could hear the wind chimes, and when the string lights broke, he kept going out there. He wrote chapter after chapter and took business calls and listened to those wind chimes, all in the middle of shattered glass. I would have been angrier about his not sweeping it up had I not been completely bumfuzzled by his ability to work in the midst of such chaos, to stick to a thought, to nail a last line while sitting in a pile of glass. I cussed under my breath and told myself I was going to see how long he could do it; however, I couldn't hold myself back long enough to outlast his singular vision. I lost my mind, and he gladly swept it up.

I swear he's going to live to be 110. As I watch him get older and grayer and more dashing, I'd be completely disgusted with him if I didn't like him so much. He's the most gifted human I know, and I mean that in the worst way possible. If he decides to write, he sits down and writes. If there is a tornado blowing through the room, he keeps writing. If he aims to read, he reads. If he decides to sleep, he drifts off.

Once in the night in that same country house, the dang dog woke us up and needed to go outside. Seth always walks the dogs at night, but this time he didn't put her on a leash, and that night, at the edge of the woods in the moonlight, there stood a goat. It bleated that I'm-a-lost-goat-in-the-night bleat, and our dog darted after it into the deep woods, so Seth sprinted after her, all the way across a couple of our neighbors' properties.

When he came back to bed out of breath, he said, "There was a goat, and Tippa chased it," and maybe five seconds later, he was snoring—after sprinting through thick, rocky Goshen woods. He was snoring, and up from my slumber, I was thinking, *A goat?! Whose goat? Where is it now? I love goats, and I think I'd like to have some. Goats make me laugh.* Small livestock keepers say that if you can slosh a bucket of water at a fence and some of the water gets through, then that fence isn't going to keep a goat in. I'm guessing that's when I started researching goat fences, while Seth slept in peace. Like with cooking, he is good at silence, and he is usually good at finding peace even when it seems impossible.

So here I am in this bedroom needing to write, and I know the boys are probably sneaking screen time. My first hurdle to silence is usually guilt, but I can sometimes skip over that to brush up on my spectacular micromanagement skills. In this case, I could be micromanaging where my children's eyeballs look. *How can I make sure they have a healthy thought life? Is that a thing? What's in their brains today?* And it's a spiral from there. *Have they been hugged enough, and are they regular?* To find silence, I have to keep myself from walking back out through the door to go ask every one of them if they need probiotics.

For me to find silence, I have to hush the deluge of list making required by mother love. I feel my jaw clench. I have to be okay with the fact that there is no plan for dinner tomorrow night, and I have to not order groceries. I cannot ask who will thaw the meat. I have to not know about the pee at the base of the toilet from all those boys, and I have to not clean it. Not only do I think of the pee, but I also think of how I'm the only one who thinks of the pee, and then I have to hurdle anger. I have to not make charts of how to get the others to engage at this level of insanity. But to be clear, this obsessive thinking, my lists and charts, my need for checkmarks and a straightened space, this is what has kept us out of disarray—or so I tell myself.

So far today, here is a list of the things I've done to resist silence. I had a business idea for one of my friends, so I messaged her. I watered every plant on our property and a few of the neighbor's plants, even though it's supposed to rain this afternoon. I toasted some shaved coconut, sprinkled some on a smoothie bowl, and put the rest in a beautiful jar. I labeled the jar and then rearranged the pantry. I double-checked our budget. I saw an indoor plant that needed to be tied up, so I went to the yard to fetch a stake, noticed tomatoes that needed to be picked, turned over the compost, remembered I had watermelon to feed the chickens, went back in to get the watermelon, and heard the washing machine buzzer go off, which meant I needed to put clothes in the dryer.

When I plan a time of stillness and listening, I often get there by first zigzagging from the front of the house to the back, inside and out again many times before I even figure out where I plan to sit down. Sitting is not my forte, and beyond that, true stillness is like exercise for me. I need to be tricked so that I don't realize I'm doing it (like with a knitting project or influenza, for example).

There's a big question here, one I obviously wish I could avoid: Why do I find it so difficult to sit in the silence and do what feels like nothing? I suppose it has something to do with my Appalachian heritage, with the fact that no one can carve out much of a livelihood on the side of a mountain without both grit and action. There's a fear in me akin to the fear of going to hell, that if I died while running idle, something bad and long-term would happen. For my people, there were animals to feed, crops to raise, odd jobs to do to bring in extra cash, and repairs to make, and much of this had to be done in the dark hours before or after school or work in the foundry. If it didn't get done, there wouldn't be enough. Maybe that's the whispering mantra in my mind, the secret code wrapped into my DNA.

I'm not sure whether I learned it from my daddy or inherited it from the hills, but I've always been a woman in motion. In the times before I entered formal ministry, I would have been considered a "high-capacity person," though comparatively speaking, I've never built an orphanage and taught a hundred children how to read while also writing a book and starting a global enterprise in my spare time like other leaders I've known. I'm no philanthropist, but I am a mama, and I have apparently self-identified as a strong, capable, action-oriented worker. If there's work to be done, I aim to get the dirtiest doing it. My pile will be the highest. My hole will be the deepest. I birthed three sons in three years, naturally. When we had our fourth, he needed medical attention regularly and required months in the hospital and then a feeding tube that I would reinsert by myself when it came out. I wrote a book with four little boys in tow. Much of this was happening while I led prayer, Bible study, or "accountability" groups. And never was there silence.

For a happy season while I was in formal ministry, I went to seminary while meeting with our priest for nearly six hours a week. I led *lectio divina*, which provided some moments of group silence, though it was a bit contrived. I wrote sermons and had multiple coffee and lunch dates with others. I made good grades and met with people in their pain and prayed with strangers on airplanes. I never balanced much; I only seesawed hard between going full blast and landing in bed with bronchitis. In the early years of all this ministry, if I couldn't find my way to silence, it had a way of finding me eventually, even if it took a bout of sickness, but somewhere along the way, I stopped finding it altogether, even in the stillness of the night, especially in the night.

When the boys went back to school for the first time after COVID hit, it had been a year and a half since I had been alone in the house. That was also the first time our oldest drove off with all my babies in one vehicle. Finally, a quiet house. A mama alone for the first time in recent memory. You'd be sweet to imagine me making a cup of tea and reading a book, but instead I was pacing the floor like a tiger, wondering whether my boys had made it to school safely. A thousand glances at the watch. The phone ringer turned all the way up. Silence?!? Maniacal laughter. It took the first couple of hours each morning for me to decide they hadn't crashed around the corner.

I had finally been afforded the privilege of being a stay-at-home mom whose kids were all in school. I had been given the space to rest and to write again, but why couldn't I? Why didn't I know how to use the quiet space? Maybe it was because every time things got quiet, when there was space to sit and rest, I felt guilty. Maybe it's because quiet is simply not in my fighting nature. Maybe it's because when quiet moments came, the worry, fear, and rage came screaming into my head and I was forced to deal with the darker stuff of my life. Maybe it's because in the silence, I have to hold that stuff up to the light, examine it, wrestle with it, feel the weight of it.

———

It's true that Seth's early days of sobriety were the opposite of silent too, and it feels right to expect such a thing on the gnarly road to healing that weaves back and forth indefinitely through grief. At first, he blared music by Sara Groves, Andrew Peterson, Christy Nockels, and Rich Mullins because their songs sounded like healing, and he'd tell you they pushed the pain of silence away. But over time, he started telling me why and how he hurt, and I would give him long hugs to keep his oxytocin levels high. The noise in his head robbed him of sleep when sleep had always been the very thing he had that I didn't. But over the weeks of new sobriety, he learned that the noise doesn't go away if you don't listen to it and deal with it, and that takes making intentional space for silence. I watched him sit in the silence night after night, morning after morning, and over time something happened. His interior spaces quieted, calmed. He learned to find inner silence. (Granted, if you asked him, he'd tell you things still get noisy from time to time.)

I long for interior stillness, and I know that comes only through cultivating silence. I also know the red flags for needing a day of silence when I see them, or rather, maybe I mean a day to face the noise so that I can make my way through it and find silence. When my anxiety spirals out of control for days on end, or if I try to get quiet and give it some time, but all I find is the deluge, that is a red flag. Constantly looping, trying to answer how we'll survive is a red flag. If my chance for quiet comes and I respond by prepping, meal planning, checking the bank account, organizing, making appointments, cleaning, and thinking through every scenario that could possibly exist so I can be prepared for it, that's a red flag. Those red flags send a message: I'm afraid of what I'll find if I silence all that noise.

When I take silent retreats, before I can do anything close to prayer or listening, I have to clear out the noise. It's best to do it in a retreat space dedicated to silence, like our local monastery, Subiaco, but I can't always take off like that. Sometimes my silent retreat takes the form of shutting off my phone and computer and leaving them in the next room. I might light a candle to call the space sacred before my soul can feel that it's so. To get to the silence, the place where my soul knows things, I have to be desperate enough to set aside what I've been writing, whatever projects that usually distract me. I have to be okay not producing something for a day. I have to be okay to feel, and I have to be okay to name some things. This plays to my strengths, because naming things can mean list making. The way I do it is with computer paper in a giant grid on the floor.

When I settle into stillness and relax my body and aim to hear my own thoughts, the deluge isn't far behind. So I sit ready with a marker to name what floods my mind. I write a title at the top of each page and usually begin with the name of each of my boys, and what might follow will be other blank pages titled things like Health; Dream to Grow Flowers; Forgiveness; Our Parents; Homebuilding; Friendships; and Marriage. If a new topic pops up, I write it on another sheet. When more thoughts flood in, if they go under one of the titles, I might write "chronic pain" under Health because sitting still reminds me that I hurt. I have to face it for a minute. I name it. I'm hurting. There's a wave of emotion. This is usually when I say shit and keep going. This reminds me of my mama, and grief shows up. I write Parents' Divorce at the top of another sheet. It goes on like this for a while. I remember being splayed out on the floor with an unfathomable number of pages. I remember asking myself and God for some grace and mercy. It's a lot.

Once the things have been named, I'm able to look at the words on the page, and this is when I begin to pray. This is when the silence comes, when visions for my good and of the love of God for my children show up. This is when I am overwhelmed with love for Seth and able to name a thing I need to take to him, work we need to do together. This is when I know how to ask for help or when I see the grace in impossible things. I see my sin, and I am lashed with heartache. In the silence, I see the path to making amends. I experience forgiveness, peace, and hope.

It may be true that some of us don't get to ask someone else to make dinner. Some of us can't go berserk on a spouse when the string lights fall. Some of us still have to walk the dogs and feed the kids and find a way to pay the bills. Some of us face the end of life alone, and others of us can't move forward without the lens of chronic pain, a noise that doesn't go away. I know that. No matter the situation, if we don't find our way to silence, especially if we're telling ourselves we can't be still or even try, we will find our way to a further crisis of mind, body, and soul. We weren't made for such churning. We were made to be known and to receive love. Psalm 149:4 says, "The LORD takes delight in his people," and I believe silence is the path to delight, the path of knowing we are small wonders to God. In the silence, we see there are small wonders he wants to show us too, gifts of divine delight.

These days, I find silence on the land, in the garden, on a walk. I look at all the seed heads blowing across the field, barely whispering. Those seeds will fall into the ground, crack open, and begin to grow, and they'll do it all in the silence. In the garden, a spider has laced a web between two tomato plants, and glass beads reflect rainbows in the morning sun. The spider spun this web in silence; the water collected in silence; the rainbow of promise glints in silence. A caterpillar inches its way across my garden, on its way to eat a leaf, and I consider just how hungry all of creation is. In the silence, my hunger is there, always so present. There, in that hunger, I remember promise and beauty. There, I remember the human condition, but I also remember the God of love who put all of this in motion. I remember that there are very good things in this life, a life of so much noise and despair. And for those few minutes, I am satisfied.

Practice: Engage Active Silence

Maybe you're a lot like Amber. Maybe you find silence difficult because of the deluge of thoughts and to-dos. That's okay. The practice of silence is just that—practice.

This week, find some time to be alone for thirty minutes. There, try your best to clear your mind and simply ask God to be with you, to show you his love. When a thought pops into your head—and it invariably will—write it down on a piece of paper, release it, and return to the silence.

When the thirty minutes are up, you may have an entire list of things that popped into your head. It's okay. Some of those things may be common annoyances, like whether or not you've paid a bill or what your calendar looks like for the next week. Some of those things, though, may be invitations to prayer.

In the silence, did financial worries intrude?

In the silence, did the name of a friend you've hurt or who's hurt you come to mind?

In the silence, did you feel the compulsion to pick up your phone and scroll your social media feed?

Spend a few minutes examining your list and asking what needs to be taken to God in prayer. But don't stop there. Make a plan to address the things that came up in the silence. Do you need to forgive someone or make amends? (We'll look at both later.) Do you need to eliminate noise or hurry from your life? Write those things down and make a plan to take action on what you learned in the silence.

six

NAME THE KNOTS

Seth: The Knots of a Father

12:00. Midnight. October 25. My birthday.

In a windowless basement of the Hilton Denver City Center, I hear familiar lyrics from my college years:

> Biggie, Biggie, Biggie, can't you see?
> Sometimes your words just hypnotize me.[1]

This is how I'm ringing in my forty-fourth year. I'm 787 miles from Amber, my four boys, the town where I've rung in every birthday for the past two decades. I'm among mountains of documents, binders, and banks of computers in a space called the war room. My friends and colleagues, Wendy and Chris, pause and sing the refrain together. Wendy is a great chair dancer, and she spares a few minutes of work to throw a seated dance party for my birthday. Chris mostly laughs and eats miniature peanut butter cups.

The last chorus plays, and Wendy asks, "Is there anywhere you'd rather be on your forty-fourth birthday?" It is a comment laced with sarcasm, but here's the truth of that moment: if I had to choose the partygoers for a working forty-fourth birthday, these would be among the very few people I'd choose.

Tomorrow we'll walk into the United States District Court for the District of Colorado, and we'll choose a jury of twelve. These twelve jury members will spend the next two months considering the United States Department of Justice's case against ten men in the poultry industry who allegedly conspired to increase corporate profits by fixing chicken prices. This, the DOJ says, was an ongoing conspiracy constituting an antitrust violation, one that impacted American consumers. A "kitchen table" issue, they say. We represent one of those men.

For months, I've considered the enormity of this case. Thousands of documents. Scores of witnesses. All those stories to keep straight. But despite the DOJ's allegations of a sprawling conspiracy, not a single alleged defendant has turned state's evidence. Not one of them has entered into a plea bargain agreeing to testify against the other defendants in exchange for a reduced sentence. And I know why. These men are certainly guilty of some everyday sins—no more than the rest of us—but they are not guilty of conspiracy to manipulate poultry prices.

In the months leading up to the trial, I pored over the documents with the rest of our team, read witness statements taken by the FBI, reviewed the confused testimony of the government's star witness—an FBI agent. Like the rest of the defense attorneys who've put their eyes on this case, I've come to a conclusion much different from the DOJ's. The conclusion: this case is utter crap. It's a pastiche of barely circumstantial evidence about a complicated commodity industry that the government just doesn't understand. But still, ten men are staring down the possibility of prison, and

I can't help but see the case as politically motivated. If the government can blame rising chicken prices on anything other than the usual suspects—inflationary policy, supply chain disruptions, COVID policy—if it can shift the blame to these ten men, then it can come off looking like the hero instead of part of the problem.

Biggie fades, and I'm back to considering the jury pool. Are there classes of individuals who'll be biased against ten white, middle-aged, male, corporate employees? Will progressive women or millennial dudes be prone to convict? What about engineers whose worlds revolve around formulas, people who don't know the first thing about the ebbs and flows of commodities like chicken? I feel a little dirty asking these questions, but this is what it means to represent an innocent man—identify and eliminate bias.

Somewhere in the early hours of the morning, my brain fogs over, so I say my good nights and make my way to my hotel room. I consider Wendy's question again: Is there anywhere I'd rather be on my forty-fourth birthday? Yes. I'd rather be at home, in my own bed. I'd rather wake to Amber, to my teenage sons mumbling, "Happy birthday, Dad." I'd rather be present, the "good dad" attending every high school basketball game and school presentation. I'd rather be helping my four boys navigate the very real and personal dramas of school, girls, and teenage bullies who believe manhood means lording power over the weak. Instead, I'm dealing with bigger bullies lording greater power over everyday people.

I fall into a bed that has been shared by countless humans, the ghosts of all those people in this room, all of us descendants of the first people, all of us living out some part of our story in this very room. In the morning, ten defendants and dozens of lawyers will leave their hotel rooms and walk into a federal courthouse. There we'll select a jury. All of them descendants of the first people too. Together, we'll write a chapter of the human struggle.

I think a lot about my sons when I'm traveling. Mostly, I think about them because it wasn't too long ago that I was their age, with their struggles, their hopes, their dreams. I couldn't quite figure out girls, and I wondered whether I'd find the one. How would I make money—musician, writer, economist? Would I make enough money? Would anyone know my name?

I wonder how I got from there to here, and I wonder what my sons' "here" will be. Will they be lawyers like their dad? Will they be artists, engineers, welders, literature professors, coaches, or, as Jude used to proclaim, "funners"? (I'm still not sure how you earn a living as a funner.) I wonder how they'll experience the world too, a world that seems to be ever in flux.

Flux is the present phenomenon, but it is not new. From the beginning, flux has been the primary characteristic of life on this planet. In the beginning, Adam and Eve ate the apple, and this gave birth to the epoch of flux. Everything changed—the understanding of good and evil, their awareness of nakedness, their relationship with their Creator. Flux was the ripple effect of their one decision. Did they see it in the moment? Did they know they'd created turmoil not only for themselves but also for their kids, their kids' kids, and so forth and so on, forever and ever, world without end?

As the story goes, God found the first humans in hiding, and after sorting out what they'd done, he granted them physical manifestations of flux. Eve's body changed, and now generations would pass through the pains of a woman. The shape of the land changed too, and now generations would be fed by the sweat of Adam's brow, but only if the rains allowed. And because I'm a man, I wonder whether Adam understood what this meant for all the man-sons who'd come after him. Did he see the millennia of his off-spring who would till the soil, slaughter the cows, punch out the parts at the factory, drive the rivets, operate the crane, perform the surgery, drill the oil wells, count the money, or write the legal briefs? Did he understand that awakening evil affected not only the land but also the human heart? Did he see brother turning against brother, lawyer against lawyer, factory worker against foreman, surgeon against cancer, et cetera, et cetera? Could he see me standing in a courtroom in Denver defending an innocent man against unjust claims brought by a government?

I wonder, too, in eating evil into the world, if the world's first people understood that they had set the conditions for slavery, colonialism, Auschwitz, the slaughter of the Tutsi, the ascendency of Vladimir Putin. Did they understand that evils would arise in our everyday lives—narcissistic pastors, spiritual abuse, and Christian cover-ups among them?

This is what I believe: In an instant, Adam and Eve knew what they'd brought into the world because they gained the knowledge of good and evil. Antagonism would lead to angst; angst would lead to turmoil; turmoil would lead to war; war would lead to despair. There, in that garden, the DNA of all humanity was tied together in a mess of inter-connected Gordian knots, and undoing those knots would require some greater force, the force of perfect obedience. At least, this is what the first Christian theologians believed.

If you get deep into church history—second-century deep—you'll meet Irenaeus, a church father who wrote to ad-dress the heresies of the Gnostics. Bodies mattered, he wrote, and so just as the disobedience of Eve set the conditions for the knots of humanity (and this is not to say Adam is off the hook), the obedience of Mary—her "yes" to carrying the

Christ—set the conditions for the undoing of those knots. In Irenaeus's cosmology, the scales of justice balance. By her disobedience, one woman tied knots into the world; by her obedience, another woman loosened them.

Irenaeus isn't alone in his cosmology. The apostle Paul wrote that in the same way the disobedience of one man (Adam) turned all of us into sinners, the obedience of Christ made us righteous. Put another way, just as Adam had tightened the knots around our hands and feet, Christ cut them loose.

I think a lot about the knots of men because Amber and I are raising four boys in a society where men are dropping like flies. This isn't just fearmongering rhetoric, nor is it a woe-is-men argument. It's a simple fact supported by the research. In 2021, the Survey Center on American Life found that 15 percent of men had no close friends—in 1990, that number was only 3 percent—and if you include those who say they have two friends or less, the percentage skyrockets to 35 percent.[2] Men (and the men of the future) are living in isolation, and that isolation has driven a crisis of deaths of despair—deaths associated with suicide or overdose. In fact, according to David Brooks, men account for almost three out of every four deaths of despair.[3] And those numbers don't appear to be getting better anytime soon. In a May 2020 report, reputable researchers looking at deaths of despair driven by COVID predicted we might lose as many as 154,000 human lives (mostly male) in the next decade, depending on the speed of economic recovery.[4]

Isolation, friendlessness, a lack of intimacy—these are not the only knots that bind up boys and men. On social media, I see strongmen decrying the feminization of society. They talk an awful lot about man codes, mock those who don't rise to their standard of "manly men." Some bros tie masculinity to their ability to grow a beard, hold their whiskey, or throw a punch. It is true that some of these men embody the classical ideals of masculinity—ultramarathon runner David Goggins comes to mind. But what signal does this send to the lanky kid, the born literature lover who's never hunted a thing in his life? The one who hates MMA, the NBA, the NFL, and any other three-lettered sporting league? Here is the message: you are not one of us; you never will be.

Then I see others claiming that "manly men" are the problem. We are colonizers, the objectifiers, the patriarchy. We have the power. There's no doubt that a lot of men have done a lot of colonizing, objectifying, and paternalizing. We've misused power too. But when society bangs this drum over and over, what message does it send to our boys, particularly the ones who love stereotypically masculine things? Here is the message: we don't need you anymore.

I look at my own sons, the ways God has made them. Two are born gym rats. Two are born artists. If they take in the prevailing messages of society, two will hear this: we do not need you. The other two will hear this: you are not one of us. Both of those messages tie me in knots. How does a father undo those knots?

These are not the only knots of men, of course. My Black friends have to warn their Black boys about the knots they've inherited. Those knots require them to instruct their sons about things many of us take for granted, things like how to walk down the street.

Don't pull your hood up.

Don't walk with your hands in your pockets.

Don't run when the police call your name.

Don't project toughness, hardness, hoodness.

The pressure of being Black in America—could this explain, at least in part, why death by suicide among Black youth has risen 60 percent in the last twenty years, a rate faster than among any other ethnic group?[5]

I'm not worried that my sons will be arrested or shot just because they happen to be walking outside after dark. I'm not worried they'll be arrested for driving with a broken taillight. But still, when I think of the plight of young men in this age—young men of all ethnicities—a sort of despair sets in. The despair of fatherhood.

I cannot help that I was born male, nor can my sons. My friend Jay cannot help that he was born Black, nor can his son. We were born into bodies with genetic codes—sex, ethnicity, muscular and intellectual potential. And all these codes come with a history of knots. If we don't name those knots, if we don't recognize their effects, what else is there but despair?

What does it mean to be a man? Some of us were created to be warriors and fighters—martial artists, soldiers, hunters, lawyers. We have bodies built for the work, psyches trained for it too. Others of us were created to be artists—painters, sculptors, musicians. We have the generative creativity of God wound into our genetic code. Some of us were born white and others Black, each with different bags to carry. But all of us were born into knots because we were born into the human family, the descendants of Adam and Eve.

How does a father carry these knots? Better yet, how does he begin to undo them? This is the deep down thing. He recognizes the purpose of his body, the body inherited from Adam but also the body Christ came in. He recognizes his potential for both grave disobedience and self-sacrificial obedience. Then he mimics the way of Christ, sacrificing his desires, his income, his everything for the sake of his family, his friends, and even his clients. And in that way, he both names the knots and allows them to be undone by his partnership with the cosmic work of Christ. In that way, he brings hope to others whose knots have tied them up in despair.

Maybe this is too technical, practical, or tactical. But if we're to follow in the way of Christ, how can we undo knots without mimicking his way?

In December 2021, the jury entered the room, told the judge they simply couldn't reach a verdict. So, we'd try the case again beginning in February of the following year. Again, I would spend an inordinate amount of time away from my family. Again, the jury would fail to reach a verdict, and it was after this second trial that the DOJ finally understood the truth, at least as to our client. There simply wasn't enough evidence to convict him.

They'd cut him loose, but they'd go on to try the case a third time against a handful of remaining defendants. And there, in that same courtroom, the jury would send a decisive verdict to the government. All those remaining men were declared not guilty. For all their posturing, all their antagonistic wrangling, all the bullying they'd done with all the taxpayer money spent, they'd get nothing.

I think about those ten men a lot these days, how knotted up they were through the years of litigation. Those knots weren't undone by their own efforts. A group of men and women said yes to representation, and through their skillful naming of the knots and their legal acumen, they set the men free. I can't help but think that this is a deep down thing too.

We've been placed in a world in flux, given bodies to navigate that flux. Sometimes we'll find ourselves tied up in knots, and we'll need the prayer and help of others to undo those knots. Sometimes we'll be the instruments of undoing. At all times, though, we know that unnamed knots will remain. It's those remaining knots that bind us up.

By knowing and naming knots, we come to see deep down things. Things like this: We were created—each of us—on purpose and for a purpose. We were given particular bodies and particular tasks. And our ultimate task? To use our bodies in self-sacrificial obedience, partnering with Christ through both prayer and labor to untie the knots that bind humanity.

Amber: On Practicing Holy Apathy

"Well, Amber, it looks like you quit smoking pot." That's what my high school librarian proclaimed over a silent room of studying students when I went back to visit after a year of college. And in that room where Corey Guffey and I used to pass sad poetry across the table, everyone laughed when I took my newfound freedom to holler in a space where I no longer had to be silent: "Mrs. Pace, I quit more than that!"

When I first came to faith, I was fiery with belief and out in the open with it. I'd been rescued, I told strangers and friends. You'd think it wouldn't have taken me—a poster child of redemption and healing—so long to see how much pain I had ignored to be able to wave my Jesus flag. I thought it was a one-and-done trade-off. My life of woe for a life of blessing; I was blind but now I see. No one told me that even though Jesus saves, I still had work to do.

After spending my late teenage years partying my brains out, I left the University of North Alabama, where I'd spent freshman year, and moved to Arkansas to secretly have an abortion. This is where I found my bottom. It's when I fell onto the floor in my dorm room and finally found my way to Jesus. And all these years later, I know that as soon as I walked out of that room, someone should have immediately carted me off to intensive live-in therapy because I had years of pain to untangle. Instead, I thought I had to believe that Jesus had rescued me from my pain, and so, my pain was gone. I believed Jesus. I disbelieved my pain—or maybe rather, I discounted it. But that's not how "salvation" works. It'd take years for me to realize that Jesus didn't erase the need for ongoing identity work and healing, which is why I didn't rise from baptismal waters walking from wave to wave, feeding the poor, and lovingly inviting small children to lead my way.

As I've grown older, I've come to see how quick I am to look at someone who's struggling and say, "You look weary. Let me carry this." But looking inward and knowing that I am weary, knowing that I'm a web of pain, shame, and knotty emotion isn't something I've found easy to do. I carry such pain sometimes that I wonder if some memories have escaped me as a form of protection. I don't know what all I've forgotten, but I do know that my shoulders are calcified from whatever it is. Most often, if I broach even the edge of my own pain, especially the underneath of it, the ache causes immediate retreat. It's easy to run from pain, but incarnating the truth of and transformation by it means taking the love of God into the darkest places, the places that make us fear and tremble (Phil. 2:12).

Catholics call this process of letting God into our darkest places "continual conversion," and something about that phrase makes me sit up in attention. "I have been saved. I am being saved. I will be saved." This is what we say, but of course, I'm still working to understand what it looks like to live this out. What little I understand of it is this: there are things within me that still need transformation, and those things need to be named.

But there's something else I'm beginning to understand too: I'm not smart enough to name everything knotted up inside me all at once. The naming happens slowly, thread by thread. These days, I'm naming that I'm not as strong as I once projected. I might look strong. I always talk strong. I walk like I have a backbone, like I'm not afraid to take up space. I carry myself like I know who I am, but the truth is I have knots disguised as muscles, and I am weak and inflamed from using my knots to carry what isn't mine to carry, what I was meant to release. Hoping to untangle these knots, I signed up for Pilates.

When I started classes, my Pilates instructor asked me to put the heel of my palms on my hips and my fingers on my pubic bone to create a triangle over my lowest abdominal muscles, what she calls my "bottom drawer." This physical touch was meant to trigger a connection to help my brain create a muscle memory as I scooped my tailbone forward to strengthen my core. I placed my hands in a triangle there between my hips, which of course was over the place I carried my babies, the place that now brings me physical grief as I creep up in age. When I made that connection there, bright, surprised tears brimmed my eyes. I was embarrassed. It was just a triangle, but there was no small amount of joy and sorrow in that bottom drawer. I wasn't even trying to find these distinguishable threads of joy and sorrow. Then I named what threads I found and put them back in the drawer as I continued articulating my spine. As I moved, a flash of light moved through me, a knot undone a little, as if the knot had been where darkness had gone to hide.

It wasn't until I named the knots in my body and then started undoing them that I discovered other kinds of knots. And this process is continual. When we undo one set of knots, we often find others. When we undo those, we find others still.

When my efforts to build muscle landed me in bed (weaker, not stronger), I realized I couldn't build muscle unless I broke down those obstructive knots. So both of my instructors advised me to make massage therapy part of my exercise regimen, and I didn't protest. Soon after, I took a trip to see some friends, and we decided to visit our host's best-kept secret—what she called her janky spa, which is the place that breaks down the knots in her shoulders and back.

The janky spa was in a run-down, near-empty mall with used-up carpet that looked like it had been the site of more than a few crime scenes. We forged ahead to an almost lovely indoor storefront with available tables inside and immediately lay facedown with our clothes on. Through the little face hole in the table, I could see that my masseuse had on a solid size 14 shoe. He was a very large man, and he proceeded to elbow through my muscles like he was trying to turn a bag of rocks into sand. Sandwiched between two of my friends, I made sounds I didn't know I had in me and breathed like I was in labor. The next day I was bruised from stem to stern. It was awful, but the knots were gone.

I wish dealing with the knots of our inner selves was as easy as this. Just find what's all balled up inside and get a giant fella to pulverize it until our souls are putty, ready to be made strong again.

When my oldest son was very young, he couldn't stop nervously tying the drawstrings of his sweatpants or shorts in knots. Before every load of laundry, there I was, untying knot after knot, wondering how he made them so complex. A few times, he couldn't even get them undone enough to go to the bathroom, so I had to stand there frantically undoing knots so he could take care of his business. This is what mothers do, isn't it?

It doesn't take a philosopher to name most of my spiritual knots. Mine have shaped me into a manager of other people's welfare and emotions, often to the exclusion of my own, because this is what I've believed has always kept me safe. When I was in the ordination process, our priest was called "father," and though women priests in the Anglican tradition aren't usually called "mother," this is exactly how it would play out. I am still a mother by vocation, but back then, in my days of ministry, I mothered by way of managing the emotions of our priest. When I mentioned the names of other ministers and those in my seminary cohort, he shared his jealousy. I protected him from parishioners so no one would have to deal with his emotions. If I confronted him about how he'd hurt me or others, he'd say he hadn't realized he'd been such a bad leader, which felt like a passive-aggressive angle for a compliment. Every time, in an effort to keep the peace, I switched to the reassuring presence he wanted, needed. And this, to say the least, knotted me up a great deal.

My greatest addiction is the one where I tell myself I'm on my own here to fix what needs to be fixed, and I excuse it by telling myself it comes from a good-natured mama heart. I don't recommend it. I don't recommend the sneaky martyrdom that needs to constantly take the temperature for loneliness and doubt, insecurity and despair, to try to assuage them. All addictions lie to us, and this one is no exception. It boasts of a backward and lonely kind of grandeur when it tells me, "It is up to you, and you are on your own here." If I don't assuage the insecurity, who will? If I don't notice it, who will? If I don't manage it, who will? I'm on my own here.

If I don't, who will—this has been my constant theme for most of my life. Though, after the last few years of healing, I'm happy to report that I now find myself leaning toward what I can only describe as holy apathy instead, when I'm more likely to hand things straight away to God without getting tangled in them. But even holy apathy hasn't helped me with some of the knots. Whatever the knot, if I can pull on a thread, it all still seems to lead to my deep desire to keep the world around me bearable and unified. Right there where the knots ache, asking me to take a look, I'm finding a deep down thing, and it is both terrible and beautiful to discover: nothing threatens control more than motherhood because mothers can't control outcomes. They can love, nurture, speak the truth—that's about it.

As I undo the knots, I'm learning that the actions of the women in our lives matter. They shape us, sometimes with misshapen care; they tighten us up in disregard; or they help us untangle the knots.

Maybe motherhood is a touchy thing for me because so many of my knots were passed down. I hunch where my mama hunches. My grandmother would look at my spine and say it was crooked like her own grandmother's. Maybe I've only made it worse by fighting and denying it instead of naming it and asking why. What was before me that made me shaped how I am?

There was a sharecropper's daughter, pregnant before marriage. The baby would one day become my mama's mama. She was discarded into the care of other family members for far too long. She grew up beautiful, making people laugh, and as soon as she could, she sneaked off to marry a boy at age eighteen. That boy was my mama's daddy, and when those kids became parents to my mama, there proved to be a lot of pain in that house.

My own mama was a miracle to me, a sweet-mouthed child at heart who trusted her own vows and believed in love even when it didn't make any sense to believe in such a thing. She was tender and not angry and worked hard and made four babies in six years, and those babies still love each other in a way that feels rare and precious. It was all a miracle. I saw and knew it, but early on, I decided I wasn't going to be wounded and scarred like her (joke's on me again). All the knots of abandonment that lived in her mother were passed to her in some not-so-passive ways.

I've always seen myself more like my daddy. Sharp and pointed, the world on his shoulders. His job was to take care of my mama, and so was mine, and it made me feel good to know that so much depended on me. I felt the need to care for her not because she wasn't a good mama but rather because she was a good mama. I didn't want anybody to hurt her again. I would lie instead of express my needs or my trouble. I didn't want her to feel sad or bad or any negative thing. So when my grandmother died, I cried for the woman who passed all those knots to a daughter I know she loved. I cried because the death of a mother should never be what sets a daughter free.

I've stood outside myself and watched me hug my mama in many healing embraces, but I don't ever remember doing it as a receiver—not that it wasn't offered. She has only ever poured out for me. The love and embraces were there. It's just that I had made a pact to always be the giver so that I wouldn't be like the ones who take, like the ones from whom so much had been taken. It's funny, though, how now I see the truth of my mama. She was the strong one. She didn't need to be protected. She needed to be let in.

When Seth and I walked the aisle, his mom was about the age I am now, and she meant everything she said, which was everything she was supposed to say. She said I was her daughter now, and I loved that idea—at arm's length. But did she know what she was saying? Did she understand she was both gaining a daughter and giving up her last child all at the same time?

Now I see how it works. Right as our kids are winding up to leave the house, perimenopause strikes us moms with little heat strokes, random secret internal panic attacks that last for weeks on end, and the realization that the house is about to be empty and we'll likely never raise another baby. Too much is coming to a yo-yoing close at once. We never know if we're pregnant or going to have a ten-day cycle or gain ten pounds for no reason whatsoever or just be so tired that we can't wear real pants anymore. Our hair turns out like proof that we have been electrocuted, but of course we can't remember what made it that way because of brain fog. Then our kids with still-developing brains get in the car and drive off with other like-minded kids. They fall in love and start coming to conclusions that are outside our sense of order, and sometimes they seem so dumb that we wonder how they get around at all, but they do. Then some girl or boy comes along and takes hold of our child's heart and moves them across the country, and they start their own family. In that moment, if we have eyes to see, we notice all the many knots we still have inside us—knots of fear, anxiety, control, maybe even the sense that we've been abandoned.

Seth's poor mother, Susan, reared a very good virgin boy who went and found an outside-of-the-box Alabama girl with a tongue ring (it was the '90s), one who had quit smoking almost everything there was to smoke only a couple months before they met. I cannot imagine the feeling that must have shot through her body when Seth told her that he wanted to buy me a diamond ring only two months after we met. And did I mention that I was nineteen? Did I mention that we planned to move to either Alabama or Oklahoma? Talk about control. There was none to be found for any of us, but especially for Susan.

Susan is tall and beautiful, much like my mama, and she inherited a sense of command and control from her daddy, who'd been a successful businessman in northern Louisiana. We are similar in many ways, had some rebellious younger years and dramatic conversion stories complete with lives that changed in the light of Jesus. We both come by command and control honestly. So many of the addictions in my family were hidden to me until I was older, but they were a little more out there with her. Her mama (Seth's grandmother) was only ever a glorious and godly queen to me, but in Susan's younger years, her mom had been an alcoholic. As a result, Susan became the caretaker, practically the mom to her brothers, and had to have control so she could manage to survive. Imagine the knots.

But about the time I came around, our matriarch, her beautiful mama, the one who had turned from the bottle and come back to Susan with healing mother love, was getting sick. She was a balm to us all, but it was cancer, and with all the authority, beauty, and clout she had, Susan couldn't stop it. It wasn't long afterward that she lost her older brother and then her strong, invincible daddy. At this point, many of us were flailing. The order of the world went irrevocably cattywampus, and Susan felt it more than any of us. I wasn't mature enough to understand it.

For years, I thought all her angst was about me and the way I'd taken her son off to live in the Ozarks. I wasn't sure if she wanted me as her daughter, though there was no doubt she loved me. Whether she or I were ready or not, she had become my mother, and her knots became mine too.

Then came a season when Susan began to name her knots. She decided to go to a twelve-step program because there were more than a few people in her life who'd had drinking problems over the years—her mother, her brother, her son—and that had worked certain knots in her. In those meetings, week after week, she began to speak the truth about her own need to manage and control, about her own knots. She took the twelve steps seriously, worked her way through them. As she named the people who'd hurt her and the people she'd hurt, and she made her amends before God and others, her knots began to unwind.

Fast-forward, leaving behind a million beautiful details, I can write that Susan is now one of my best friends. Things fell apart for us for a season, but we decided together that we loved each other. We made and kept boundaries together. Then I watched her go off and do work I hadn't understood she needed to do. It wasn't work that uncovered how bad she was, because she wasn't. Instead, the work revealed that it was worth the work to be free of nameable knots. I watched this beautiful woman name her knots, and slowly, with God, they unraveled.

Unexpectedly, Susan untied knots in my own life. She looked inward and apologized, which released me enough to let her in, to see how stiff-armed I'd been with her and other women in my life. Watching her do her own work is one of the greatest ways anyone has ever helped me do mine. And now, years later, I can say that our relationship is proof that even the trickiest knots can be undone. Watching her do the work gave me hope and helped me realize that it's not too late for my body or for the way I react to my own kids. These knots were never meant to remain.

In the same way Susan did the work to undo her own knots, I began meeting with a spiritual director named Elizabeth, who's helped me work to undo mine. She's helped me name the knots created in relationship with the priest, with my own mother, and with my role as mother. Of course, the work of naming knots is never done, since I have continued to remain human. I am still in my conversion story. I still need help.

It stands to reason that when I was considering Catholicism, our Lady—Mary, the mother of Christ—gave me the most trouble. Is she really our mother? Did Jesus really mean it for all of us when he told St. John in the midst of his passion to behold her as mother? It was a sweet idea, and that's how she stayed with me: a sweet idea of the meek mother who prays for us along with all the other saints. I was taught that she cares for us and only ever points us to Jesus, and that was beautiful enough of an idea for me to get along with it cognitively.

Over time, in the Adoration Chapel, rosary in hand, I asked God what I was missing about Mary. Why didn't I feel that she was my mother? Why couldn't I get it down deep? The answer felt like a boulder dropping out of nowhere. I heard a crushing truth: "You've never let yourself be mothered."

I didn't ask myself until my forties if I could ever let someone mother me. I was a full-grown woman who'd mothered boys and grown men alike before I asked God to help me allow myself such pleasure. I prayed a half side-prayer that if Mary really was my mother, would she show herself to me, and once I asked for it, I felt desperate, as if I'd tied myself up in my own pants and couldn't get out. I wanted her face to appear on a piece of toast, her apparition to appear at my bedside, her robe to drop flowers at my feet. She must have joined in the prayer because even though I haven't seen her with my eyes, I see her everywhere nonetheless. An image of her sacred heart with seven swords on my wall, bluebells by the roadside, her image on a bread truck in Santa Fe. I have seen her time and again, and when I do, I ask her to help undo my knots through her intercession. If the faithful saints cheer for us as we run the race, as Hebrews 12:1–11 describes, then their cheers are living prayers, and Mary is Queen Mother in the midst of them. Her cheers are the watchful prayers of a mother. I'm finding that when I ask her to pray, I'm more able to name the knots, which go quickly to her Son. And naming those knots and feeling them loosen up makes space for the love of God to come into those darker places and bring something like conversion.

———

Our family has become repeat visitors to Santa Fe, because of its unending art and food and because of the topography of the surrounding area. We love to attend Mass at the basilica and hear its echoing bells. We walk through the prayer garden along each of the stations of the cross. St. Frances opens his arms, shaped like wings, in joyous dance on water at the Cathedral Park. The labyrinth with the statue of St. Kateri Tekakwitha and sometimes even a parade of parishioners dressed as biblical characters, chanting their subversive prayers (signs that say "stop gun violence" after Uvalde), make the basilica a place of welcome for the wanderer, the hurting, and the weary.

I wind through each of these images and find my way to the statue of Mary, Undoer of Knots. Of course, I'm drawn to her again. On her head is a crown of stars, and beneath her feet are the moon and a snake. She holds a long ribbon full of knots, but the snake itself is tied in a knot, and she's standing strong over its body, pinning it down. I am closer to the level of her massive feet and wonder if she stands so strong there waiting for her Son to come and crush its head.

What would she have me do? Standing under that sculpture of my powerful and tender mother, I want her to show me things: how to let a son go; how to remember my first received identity—daughter; how to feed and nurture; how to intercede; how to let myself be mothered. And there, somehow, the knots release a little more; there's a little less room for the darkness to hide. There's a tighter knot in the tail of that snake.

Practice: Name the Knots

So often when despair sets in, we have a hard time naming exactly why. We find ourselves anxious, in fear, wound up in knots. How do we name those knots? A better question: How do we loosen those knots?

God has given many the gift and the vocation of helping others name and loosen knots. (What could be a better deep down thing than God's love expressed through human gifts?) That person may be your priest or pastor. But for some knots of despair, you might need the help of a therapist, counselor, spiritual director, or addiction specialist. If you're having trouble saying exactly what the trouble is, make an appointment with one of these people. If you don't have a priest, pastor, or therapist, ask a friend who does. Find someone who can help you name the knots and begin to unravel them.

You could also ask for prayers from the saints, maybe even from the heavenly mother. She's pretty helpful with knots. But if that's uncomfortable (we totally get it), ask a friend or maybe even your own mama to pray for you.

seven

MAKE AMENDS

Seth: The Thing about Reconciliation

I was in Grand Rapids for the audiobook reading of *The Book of Waking Up* when I received the news. The church—the one we'd called our community for five years even though we hadn't attended in over three months—was finally sharing the news of our priest's departure.

As in anything, the devil is in the details, and these are those details. Amber had withdrawn from her curacy weeks before and had written a letter to the diocese (the body governing a set of churches) sharing her experiences with the priest. The diocese had employed a third-party investigation headed by a man I'll call the director, who led the team examining the case. I was told the director was a priest, but here's what I did not know at the time: he was a diocesan priest who attended the congregation headed by the dean, the bishop's administrative right hand.

After the investigation, the director and his team issued their report, which was deemed property of the diocese and not to be shared with us. Some believed we were entitled to see the findings—they dealt with Amber's lived experience, after all. So we read that report, and to say it painted the relationship between the priest and Amber in a negative light is no small understatement. There were admissions, findings, and hard recommendations. There was a recognition of the power dynamic of a relationship that was unhealthy. Still, the conclusions were gray. Neither the third party nor the diocese called what happened spiritual abuse, because the director of the investigation indicated that it was impossible to access the thoughts and intentions of another man's heart—as if discerning abuse requires mind reading. And if the diocese wouldn't call it abuse, how could the church? So, without any findings of intent to abuse, the narrative die was cast.

The devil is in the details, but here's the ragged truth: none of the details of the report were shared with the congregation because the diocese had directed the vestry to keep those findings quiet. Amber's story was never shared. The church never addressed why Amber (the curate in the ordination process) and I (who led music from week to week) had disappeared. And then the coup de grâce: they dismissed the priest but didn't call it a firing. Instead, they crafted a more neutral message at the direction of the diocese: it was time for the priest to transition, and the church wished him the best.

The age-old story had played itself out. Without any plan of reconciliation with those who'd been hurt (both us and others), the church and the diocese that governed it had protected the reputation of the priest.

The message was sent to us by one of the vestry members, and Nicholas, the vestry warden, was copied on that email. Nicholas and his wife were the church planters, the founders, and two of our closest friends. I read those best-wishing words and my nerves caught fire.

We scheduled a call, and not too long after, Nicholas, the other vestry member, Amber, and I were on the phone. I can't recall the specifics of that call, and maybe those specifics don't matter much. Here's what's important to know: I took my anger off the leash. Nicholas met dog with dog, anger with anger. He was trying to keep a church together, he said. He was trying to minimize the fallout. He put the question to my head like a gun: Won't you ever be satisfied?

Satisfaction. Is this what the aggrieved want? The spiritually abused? Is there some grand retributive moment when the crushed woman rests her head on her pillow and whispers a euphoric "Oh yeah . . . he got what he deserves, and it feels so good." No, there is no satisfaction for those who carry the pain of spiritual manipulation or abuse. It's that very lack of satisfaction that defines the contours of what they really want—a heartfelt, uncoerced apology and, if not that, justice.

I recounted the facts, the things told to us in private. The vestry had heard our story and seemed to understand. Nicholas claimed to believe Amber, and the entire vestry agreed that it was time for the priest to go. Still, he wouldn't be called to account, at least not publicly. The gospel demanded repentance, I said, and, if not that, justice. There had been no repentance, and this, I said with no small amount of certainty, was not justice.

I do not remember how the call ended, only that I found myself in bed in a fitful sleep. There were visions of violence. Fire. Fists. Finger-pointing. Bile burned its way up to my mid-chest before the sun came up, and as I climbed out of my hotel bed in the dark and cold October, I felt the pull to the place of peace. I showered, dressed, and pointed my car in the direction of the Cathedral of St. Andrew in downtown Grand Rapids.

In the opening moments of the Mass, I recited these words: "I confess to almighty God, and to you, my brothers and sisters, that I have greatly sinned. In my thoughts and in my words. In what I have done. In what I have failed to do." In the recitation, I imagined Nicholas, the one I'd raged against just twelve hours before. Maybe my anger was justified, but was my mercilessness?

After the prayers, the congregation sang their alleluias and the priest took to the lectern. "The Gospel according to Luke," he said, and we crossed our heads, lips, and heart.

> In those days he departed to the mountain to pray, and he spent the night in prayer to God. When day came, he called his disciples to himself, and from them he chose Twelve, whom he also named apostles: Simon, whom he named Peter, and his brother Andrew, James, John, Philip, Bartholomew, Matthew, Thomas, James the son of Alphaeus, Simon who was called a Zealot, and Judas the son of James, and Judas Iscariot, who became a traitor. (Luke 6:12–16 NABRE)

There in the story were the forefathers of my faith, the men whom Christ collected as acquaintances, acquaintances who became friends, friends who became brothers. Simon Peter, a Jewish zealot who loathed Roman occupation. Matthew, a tax collector in league with the occupiers. James and John, actual brothers who tried to make Jesus pick which one of them was his favorite (at least that's my interpretation of the story in Mark 10:35–37). All the disciples were collected in that short passage, the men who would break out in an argument over who would be the greatest (Luke 9:46–48). These men were called into a fraternity, and like any other fraternity, it did not come without hazing, turmoil, and more than a few relational rifts. It did not come without fist fights, I'm sure.

I imagined myself there, standing on the outside of the disciples' camp. There is Peter in a foaming diatribe about the occupying Romans and the traitorous politicians and taxing officials who keep them in power. Hand on the hilt of his sword, full of a nationalist's fire, does he look across the coals at Matthew? Does he demand the former tax collector repent of his sins? There is Matthew, a recovering survivalist. He shifts on his hips, looks down, says there are things some do to keep a nation breathing, to give it a chance to fight another day. "It's better to build Caesar's chariots than to be run over by them," he says under his breath, drawing in the dirt with a stick. And in this argument, where is Jesus? I can almost see him reclining by the side of the fire, reciting the prayer he's taught these brothers: "Forgive us our sins, as we forgive everyone who sins against us."

Forgive the men you accuse of being traitors, Peter. Forgive the nationalists who accuse you of being a traitor, Matthew. Make amends with one another. Repair the breach and make way for God's reparative work in your own life.

This is a deep down thing: we are members of an odd family. There is celebration, service, and joy in that family, and in that family, we meet Christ all together at the eucharistic table. But there's a counter-truth. Disagreement, struggle, political misunderstanding, complete lack of understanding, vice, narcissism, abuse—these poison the family. There are traitors, fiends, and thieves who slip in among the family too, and sometimes, particularly in our wrath, it's difficult to distinguish friend from enemy. But friend or foe, it does not matter. Christ—the Divine Love—asks us to forgive, forgive, forgive, and in that way, we set ourselves free from that poisonous wrath.

Before leaving Grand Rapids, I sent an email apologizing for my words, but I quietly extended forgiveness too. These are impossible waters to navigate, and in that cathedral, I understood that Nicholas and the vestry were doing the best they knew how, even if it fell short of my own expectations. He accepted my apology, said there would be more to discuss later because exchanging words of forgiveness does not automatically repair the breach, particularly a breach that's attached not just to a relationship but to a local congregation, a diocese, an entire structure that pulled the chasm into place. It's a breach that opened before I uttered a word, one that opened wide when the diocese directed the church not to share the report. This, I know, is a breach that might take years to heal.

We'd like to make forgiveness tidy, and we sum it up with phrases like "forgive and forget." But is forgetting the fire an option once you've been burned? Or is forgiveness more like this: I see the fire; the fire has hurt me; I hold no grudges against the fire, but I'd rather like to avoid it. Forgiveness allows us to see the fire for its potential—the potential to burn—without hating it. Or, to put it a little more on the nose, it allows us to see those who've burned us without wishing them harm. As the poet Buddy Wakefield puts it, "Forgiveness is for anybody who needs safe passage through my mind."[1]

But here's the eternal question: Are forgiveness and reconciliation the same thing? Once you extend forgiveness, does this mean the breach is repaired? Some believe this to be true. "If you've forgiven," they say, "why not sit in the same room with your abuser? Why not tell him you release him?" To this I say: release without reconciliation is no release at all, and reconciliation requires work from the ones who've wrought the wrong.

In her *New York Times* bestselling masterwork on racial reconciliation, *Be the Bridge: Pursuing God's Heart for Racial Reconciliation*, Latasha Morrison examines reconciliation from a deeply Christian perspective. As a Black woman who'd spent a lifetime suffering under the hidden truths and half stories of historical discrimination, she'd set out to answer this question: What would it take to repair the breach between white Christian communities and their Black and Brown brothers and sisters? Her answer: nothing short of true, justice-oriented reconciliation of biblical proportions.

What does justice-oriented reconciliation look like according to Morrison? It's both give and take, and it requires work from both abused and abuser. As Morrison writes, for true reconciliation to happen, those who caused, contributed to, or benefited from the harm must become aware of how their actions caused pain. But awareness isn't enough. They must acknowledge that pain, lament their part in it. They must turn from the harm too, repent of it, and take steps to make sure it never happens again. Then they must do the work to repair the breach. (Morrison uses *repair* instead of the term *reparations* but is quick to admit the terms are interchangeable.) And just as true reconciliation cannot happen without this deep work, neither can it happen if the hurt ones don't extend radical forgiveness.

I had the privilege to work as an editor on *Be the Bridge*, and through that work, Latasha mentored me in the art of reconciliation. In that mentorship, I understood a small part of the profound pain experienced by the Black church. They'd done their best to forgive their abusers, but each time they tried, their white brothers and sisters heaped more abuse on them. They went out of their way to share this cycle of hurt too, but they could not force the white church to acknowledge, lament, repent, or take steps to repair the breach. (And no, virtue signaling support for the Black community is not the same as repairing the breach.) So, reconciliation between the Black and white churches was slow, happening only in small pockets where the Spirit instigated deep, soul-searching work of reconciliation that was accompanied by acts of repair by the abusers.

Latasha taught me that forgiveness is an imperative, but you cannot force reconciliation. Put another way, I had no Christian choice but to forgive the priest, the church, and the diocese for the way Amber's story was handled. But could I make any of them acknowledge the harm, lament it, repent of it, and repair the breach? The history of the Black church answers the question. No one can force anyone to do any-damned-thing, especially the sweaty work of reconciliation.

———

God hovers over the world, huddles over his children. He collects us together, asks us to see each other in all our wrecked humanity. Together, we are a frail family, and in us is buried the deepest-down thing in all of nature: love. Exercising that love in forgiveness, in acknowledgment, in lament, in repentance, in repair is the most difficult of all commands. And still, isn't it the thing that brings hope?

By December, the priest had flown the coop. Over burgers, I told my friend Joseph that I carried little hope that the priest, the church, or the diocese would enter into the humbling work of reconciliation. There was hope, though, that Nicholas would do the work, even if it took five years, a decade, whatever. Joseph asked what made me so sure, and I said, "It's just a hunch."

Time passed, a pandemic set in. We were confined to our homes, required to wrestle with ourselves in new ways. Some gave in to vices. Others took to soul searching. Nicholas, it seems, was in the latter category.

Over the lunch hour, he called, said he'd been thinking through the last year. But he hadn't just been thinking. He'd been doing work. He'd set out to learn more about spiritual abuse, about what it looks like and how it plays out in congregations, because he wanted to understand whether Amber's experience fit in the category. He'd read articles and books, Chuck DeGroat's book, *When Narcissism Comes to Church*, among them. He'd listened to podcasts on church abuse by Scot McKnight and spent time listening to Diane Langberg, an expert on narcissism and abuse. He'd engaged the work, and it had changed him. Then he said three simple words that bridged the gap: "I believe Amber." He asked whether I thought he could come sit with her in the backyard and talk things out, and those three simple words paved the way for my answer: "Of course."

I wasn't there when they sat in the backyard, so I'm not a firsthand teller of truth. But here are the contours of that conversation, at least as I understand them: He acknowledged his part in the rift, lamented it, said he'd work to make sure it could never happen again in that little church family, and would do whatever it took to make things right. Amber passed her forgiveness to him. But for the pandemic, they would have hugged it out. But the meeting wasn't a cure-all. The dark cloud that hung over Amber didn't disappear overnight. But amends were made, and those amends made space for healing.

Here's what I can say about Nicholas months removed from that initial conversation: He's committed to the long-term work of repair and restoration, and he has continued to listen, learn, and step into Amber's pain and the pain of those like her. He's using his voice to advocate for Amber, a woman who wasn't heard when she shared the truth of her experience, a woman who was voiceless when her abuser returned to a position of public ministry. And to be super clear, when I say Nicholas is "using his voice," I don't mean he's spouting theological constructs on Twitter about the ways men and women should relate to one another so the applauding masses will think he's on the right side of history. Instead, he continues to use his voice in quieter ways, ways that pave pathways of hope.

Here's what I can say about Amber and me: We hold no ill will toward that church and their new priest—a priest we love and admire—even though, as of the writing of this book, there's been no direct reconciliation with that church or the diocese. There's hope for reconciliation with both the church and the diocese, but even if that hope proves fruitless, we'll carry on.

Finally, here's what I can say about all of us: There are times when despair comes into our lives uninvited; there are other times, though, when we play a part in creating despair, when our words and actions pull a suffocating blanket over our family members. There, we are given a choice. We can allow our egos, our need to be right, our frightful fragility, our power, our "lack of intent," or even our processes to shield us from the deep work of repentance. Or, we can lay ourselves bare and do what love requires, pushing into the work of making amends and restoring the family. Nicholas chose the latter, and in that choosing, he was the first fruit of hope.

Amber: Holy Shit

When I was small, our land in north Alabama rolled up the mountain from the Tennessee River. What wasn't field was covered in giant oaks and pines, and the woods had long been untouched, except for the deer and squirrels and our own country play. The decomposing soil beneath the understory was black, and to put it in the garden meant to grow giant plants. Tree stumps blossomed with mushrooms, and leaves covered artifacts from both ancient and recent history. There were calcified mussel shells, shark teeth, indigenous clay beads, sometimes even shards of fancy bone china brought from overseas long ago. Rusted metal tools turned up from almost every dig. My parents had found jugs there too, what the moonshiners had left behind. It was the ground that told me I was surrounded by story. Everything felt mythical and haunted, and even the people who stood right in front of my face felt that way to me. It didn't matter how much of their history or story they told me. I knew there was more hidden beneath.

My daddy has always been a storykeeper and storyteller. He is a looming presence at six foot six, and I was tiny, so he leveled us out a little by sitting beside me on the hill above our place. He would tell me to sit still and listen, then he'd name the trees that shook around us. He told me God made the stars. God made the moon and the bobcat, the whip-poor-will, the raccoons, the strawberries, and all the good guard dogs. He made cedars for fence posts, or he made them fall and rot so we could light our fires. He made pecans for pie. Wasn't he good? God made the ground and all the water in the whole world, and it was our biggest job to follow him and to care for what he gave us. I believed him. Sitting on the hill with my mythically large daddy, it was easier for me to believe in a Creator than it was for me to believe in a man-sized catfish, and I knew those things were plentiful down in that river.

As I aged, when I saw injustice and asked my questions, he would sit and tell me that one day soon, Jesus would come back, and wrongdoers who didn't repent would get their due. The ones who really followed Jesus would be restored. Everything stolen would come back. Everybody separated would reunite. Nobody would cry anymore, and everybody would be so glad that we'd sing with perfect sound. Imagine the harmony. It's coming. Jesus will make all of this right. This is what he said.

Now as an adult, I see that my basic understanding of the grand story of this world—the beginning and the end—is about as simple now as it ever was. I don't have all the details.

I don't know what parts are scientific fact, if allegory is involved, or if we're just characters in some great literary event that is written in the stars, but I believe creation happened by God's own pointed hand. He made us good and set us free, and when our choices went cattywampus, he made a way for us to get back to him. He did that by becoming as familiar with our pain as he possibly could. He went to the dust for us, and everyone who receives that divine sacrificial love will be renewed, and those who don't believe such love could exist won't have what they need to make good of their time on this earth. I believe this is a cosmic story, and also infinitesimal. We interact with it on a daily, molecular, systemic, and intimate level. This story is in the sky and it's in my garden right now. It's in my coffee and my bank account.

Whether you believe the creation story is myth or scientific fact, whether you think the book of Revelation is about long-ago events or what is to come or an early version of some outstanding sci-fi dream, I want to tell these stories together again—the beginning and the end—in light of what we know of the ground and our role in caring for it. Wherever you are in the process of belief about Scripture, the one thing I know that is true, beautiful, and important about it is that the Bible is a story. It is literature. In fact, it's a combo-package deal of many different kinds of literature, and if God ever breathed anywhere, it would have to have been on such a book.

In light of that, I'll take a stab at retelling the beginning and the end together. It will be overly simple and probably short-sighted in a few places, but this is how I hear the story.

In the beginning, the boy—was he boy or man?—first knew himself in a garden. Everywhere there was beauty, and he was part of it. Perfection everywhere, and he didn't know any better. All the air was God's breath, and what was made was from the soil. Anywhere there was to walk was the artful presence of the divine. The boy in his garden was only ever left to the soil, which was not abandonment but rather relationship and nourishment, his being given to the place of his making. The ground was as familiar to him as his own body, and so he slept there as at the breast of the one who fed him. If God's breath fathered, it was the earth that mothered. God breathed into the dust and made man. So when God instructed Adam to work the garden and take care of it (Gen. 2:15), there are hints of love here, a relationship: receive care and nourishment from the soil and give her care in return.

In the beginning, the snake convinced Adam and Eve to consume what wasn't theirs to eat, and they all received consequences for it. To the snake: you'll eat the dust. To the woman: your labor, the work you have to do, will nearly break you, and you'll wish you had the job of the man. To the man: you will sweat to eat. You will work the ground until you return to it. You are but dust. The snake will crave you.

We have to zoom way out before we can come back in. We go from the dust of the beginning to the cosmic realm of stars at the end. In Revelation 12, there is another boy, a son, not yet born to a great mother. She is clothed with the sun, has a crown of stars on her head and the moon beneath her feet. As she goes into labor, an enormous red dragon with crowns and horns on his seven heads wipes a third of the stars away to try to get to this baby, who is Jesus. The stars fall from the sky, stardust turned to the ground. The dragon stands right by the woman in labor, because all he wants to do is gobble up that baby boy. He is insatiably hungry for this one shining boy who will be a mighty ruler, the one whose people had come from the ground, but as he's born, the baby is snatched up to God and his throne, and in a great fury, the dragon wages war. Heaven meets hell in combat, and the dragon is defeated, is hurled back to the earth, where he lives again under the ancient curse—you'll eat the dust of the earth; you'll eat and eat and eat, and you will never get the feeling of being full.

How is it that I relate so much to the snake? Am I a child of the insatiable one? That accusing dragon would have me think so, would have me think I can never be full.

I often forget the effects that the Genesis curse has on the ground. Not only would women produce children through pain, but the earth itself would experience its own pains, bearing thistles and thorns, if we don't tend to it with great care. If we work it too hard or overproduce a certain crop or overconsume its nutrients, it turns into a great dust bowl. I sometimes forget that our role isn't to consume the earth but to care for it, to make it fertile, and when needed, to amend it. Soil is a very sacred thing, and we are its children. We get to eat from it and learn what it means to restore what the devourer only consumes.

In the season of Lent, which also begins this way, in dust and ashes, the priest reminds us, "You are but dust." It is a matter of life or death that we understand this, and what a miracle it is that God entered this dusty experience through the groaning of Mary. And now Jesus gives himself to us in the bread of his table, formed from grain grown in a land somewhere that required care, dirty hands, and so much repair to the ground. It takes amendments to the soil to grow good grain, and somehow those who work the land participate in a miracle, the making of satisfying food.

Zooming back to the present, this all reminds me of the time I was convinced I would become a shepherdess instead of pastoring in church. While the young people I knew were getting importantly worked up about climate change and its impact on the oceans and animal populations, I began doing my own middle-aged work in the realm of earth care, though that's not what I intended to do. I intended to become a shepherdess—as one does. I was no longer leading a church, and that fact made me prone to bouts of crying, but sheep made me laugh. It was that simple: I wanted to shepherd sheep as a cure to tears and a way to do the thing I felt called to do, which was to lead the ones I love to good food.

So, we bought land; I planned to amend the land with stuff that made it more fertile; I wanted a relationship with the land. And all of this was so I could care for sheep and so those sheep could make weird sounds, have stupid cute babies, and make me laugh. Yes, I realize how dumb this sounds. Yes, I know sheep also disobey, run away, gouge you with horns, and die for no apparent reason.

My obsession with being a shepherdess led me to read a book called *Holy Shit*, by the late Gene Logsdon. Logsdon was once a seminary student too and had plans to be a priest, just like I had. He was the friend of Wendell Berry, Joel Salatin, and countless other stubborn farmers across the United States. *Holy Shit* is his masterwork on the subject of poop, why it's important to our entire well-being and how to better use the poop near you. There's an entire section on how to handle a manure fork so you can best sling poop where it needs to go. It's not a book of metaphors, or it didn't intend to be, but alas, holy shit, too, is sacramental—a deep down thing.

This book talks of what great lengths we go to hide ourselves from the unseemly, the dirt of us. We're a culture of multiple courtesy flushes. Feedlots are known for their stench, and bazillions of dollars are spent a year to keep that smell to a minimum so as to make doubly sure that we'll keep consuming. All the while, what was once fertile land is being zapped year after year by the modified crop. We remove the habitat that once fed it—livestock that grazes and then poops and then rotates away from the land to let it rebuild—and instead we make unnatural additions to the soil that further remove us from our relationship with the land. So often, the only thing that feeds the soil these days is low-performing fertilizer that disrupts all kinds of ecological processes that I am not smart enough to address here. But I can see with my eyes that we're becoming fools wearing white gloves, denying our mother what she needs and telling everybody that we don't poop or, if we do, that it doesn't stink.

Logsdon declares that poop is holy. We need it as part of our process of being healthy and whole, and so does the land. If the land isn't receiving nourishment, the process of planting, reaping, and replanting is its own form of nonconsensual consumption. It wears a land out. It is not communion.

I learned a lot from reading Logsdon and others about what soil actually needs. It needs us to be close to it and to feed it, to not rape it, and to not be afraid of it. It needs us to make amends with it when it's been used up because we are part of a big life circle (cue *The Lion King*). Our own actual poop and the poop of animals are what feeds the land that in turn feeds us. This is how I came to believe that small farms with rotating livestock may just save the world: the poop of that livestock mends the land and, in that way, repairs it.

Since my eyes were opened to this, I see how it applies to everything in my life. I see a church that miraculously still exists with its goodness intact in spite of two thousand years of repeated foolishness and nonconsensual consumption. How does the church remain intact? Along the way, some humble people—saints—have come in and amended her soil. They've taken that church back to the roots of true communion. Some have seen the harm done within its walls and have worked to make amends.

I have also seen how the metaphor applies to my particular situation too. I have only begun processing pain with the ones who hurt me, but as we don't avoid the shit, as we make our own amends, I am witnessing restoration, even if it's slow. Some things take time to compost. That's how the shit works, though, isn't it? The slow-breaking, deep-feeding stench of it all has done wonders to my creativity, something that left me altogether in my two years of "ministry."

Sometimes making repairs is just picking up a hoe and working hard at the compost pile, breaking up the clumps so it can all break down together. That's the whole point, the breakdown, where nothing is wasted. Not the eggshells, the onion peels, the blisters, the anger, the diminished parts of our stories, the grief. I work the compost as an act of hope because sometimes hope needs a little participation and maybe, too, a whole lot of grit.

I've never felt such broad-spread global chaos as I do this day, but since we are people of the New Adam and children of the New Eve, we can remember that God breathes in low places and made even our own stench to feed this earth. We can't ignore the shit or that we are but dust. We groan when the soil does because when the earth begins to ache, we go hungry. So when we amend the soil, we heal ourselves. Amending the soil produces our food, our bread, our wine, and points back to the God who created them. It reminds us of the dragon too, who wants to devour, deplete, and ultimately consume not only our land but also us. Amending the actual soil reminds us that the soil of friendship, family, church, and communion is repaired by making amends.

"It's all connected." When Nicholas came to my garden to ask for forgiveness, this is what he said. Nicholas and I share a temperament. He's not one for inaction, and he's not afraid of hard work on the land. On his plot of land, he moves rocks and plants grasses to keep his soil in place. He removes invasive plants in his woods, and he works at companion planting. He is a master gardener and has worked to know how all the natural world works together, how everything is connected. It's easy to think that the work of one man on a rocky hillside doesn't matter. It's a giant hill and he is an ant, working for beauty while the rest of the ant colony goes about not paying attention, not healing, not listening to the deep down things.

Nicholas didn't simply tend to the landscape outside his house, though. He read books and did the work to understand the harm, to understand his part in the harm, to name the harm, and to figure out how to make amends. Over time, he sorted out what it meant to aim for reconciliation, even as other individuals, the church as a whole, and the diocese didn't share his aim. I guess you could say he studied the soil, asked what it needed, then moved rocks and planted relational grasses to keep us from washing away altogether. It's the deep down things, the great story of this earth and how it needs amends, that informed his actions. It's all connected, he said, and he went on to share that healing one part of the earth helps the whole system work. He was one man doing what he could of his own little part to heal the earth, and now, to heal our relationship. Maybe these things would make the system just a little healthier.

What Nicholas did is all any of us can do. Stop consumption, just for a moment. See the soil—*really see it*. Notice the depletion. Understand our part in that depletion. Make repairs. Don't stop making them. It mattered to me that day in the backyard. It strengthened my backbone, helped me stand a little straighter under the weight of grief. It gave me hope then. It gives me hope still.

Practice: Repair What's Broken

The devourer would like to gobble up everything God created—soil, animals, humans. We've been created in God's image, though, which means we've been created not to consume everything but to tend to it, to create the conditions for growth, and where there's been damage, to repair it. Repairing things is not always easy, particularly when it comes to human relationships. But human as you are, there's probably someone in your life who could stand to hear a reparative word. In the same way we repair the soil by asking, "What does it need?" take some time to meditate on what that person might need. Do they need to hear from you face-to-face? On the phone? Do you need to write a letter to them?

It is one thing to be forgiven. It's another thing altogether to make repairs. Making amends is more than just apologizing. How will you communicate your willingness to change, to bring repair to the relationship? Know this too: the person you hurt may not need to hear from you. As step 9 in AA teaches, we should "make direct amends to such people wherever possible, *except when to do so would injure them or others*."[2] If this is the case, consider this advice from the Hazelden Betty Ford Foundation for making amends when there is a risk of reinjury: "We can make amends in a broader sense by taking actions like donating money, volunteering our time or providing care."[3]

Make a plan to make specific amends to the ones you've harmed. If you're not sure how to go about it, or if you're concerned that reaching out may cause reinjury, speak with a pastor, priest, or therapist about how to best go about making things right. Then commit to making amends within the week.

eight

SEARCH FOR EPIPHANIES

Seth: Go to the Sacred Spaces

I entered the National Gallery with no small amount of moaning. Only ten, I most appreciated the full-color comics in the Sunday paper—I was a Garfieldian—and this was no comics spread. The walls were impossibly white, and paintings hung as islands, each with a small card describing the artist, year, subject matter, meaning . . . who cares, whatever. There was a statue in one room, a two-foot-tall naked woman with an arched back. Some famous Russian egg across the room reflected the white lights aimed at it. Or maybe that was at a different gallery on a different occasion. Who can remember any of the boring gallery visits of youth?

This I remember without equivocation, though. Passing landscapes, portraits, the busts of people I didn't recognize, we rounded a corner, and before entering a large room, my mother stopped, leaned down, and said a name I'd never forget—Andrew Wyeth—and she followed it with another—Helga. Some of these paintings would be nude, she said. If it made me uncomfortable, I could look away, though she did not say exactly where I should look.

In the room, I saw her. The woman on a stool. On a bed. In front of a tree. Her face angular. Her body, less so. It is the body I remember most, the way the light bent around it, the way it must have bent under the brush. But it wasn't the light or the brush that caught my attention. It was the woman.

I was only ten, a boy who better understood the art of a baseball card than that of an oil painting. Still, I guessed something about Wyeth's painting and his subject. He was not simply a painter. She was not simply a subject. They were collaborators, storytellers. They had known each other. He translated each hair, pulled individual strands from a pony-tail to tell a story. He gave voice to the light that exposes and the shadow that obscures. In the exposure, Helga was vulnerable, known, explored, and it was this knowing that turned my childhood cheeks pink. Sometimes, even now, I am still that child.

Helga was the first nude woman I remember seeing. Even more, though, Helga was an introduction to epiphany. She whispered, "There are some things you cannot unsee, some things that follow you forever." That epiphany is forever pegged to a particular time, a particular place, and a particular woman. I was ten. I was in the National Gallery. I was in love with Helga.

Epiphany—a manifestation of something transcendent, something outside of us. The summer of Helga was the summer of epiphany, and that culminated in a different sort of epiphany, one tied to a different sort of place.

On the first day of my first year at Catholic school, I wandered into the sanctuary, a confused Baptist with a virgin nose to incense. There was what appeared to be a birdbath by the door, and the girl in front of me dipped her finger in it before crossing herself. I passed the pool, eyes fixed on my feet, figuring it was better to ignore what I didn't know than to do something foolish.

The sanctuary held a sort of haze, and shards of sun highlighted individual particles floating through it. The sky-blue ceiling was dotted with gold dots. Stars maybe? In single-file fashion, the class of which I was the newest member made its way into the designated pews. Each student knelt before entering the pew. I shuffled in and sat while my neighbors knelt in prayer.

Students filtered in through three entrances. Each wore a white polo shirt over khaki pants or a plaid skirt, and each understood the pool of water, the sign of the cross, the way to kneel before entering the pew, the way of silent prayer. Maybe each was too familiar with the crucifix and the statutes of the lady and man flanking the altar too, because they paid no more attention to the three than they might the furniture in their grandmother's house—outdated, uninteresting. I could not stop staring at those statues, though, couldn't help noticing something like sadness in the stone.

A man in a robe walked into the aisle, smiling. "Welcome," he said. "Remember the response to the psalm? Practice one time," he said, and two hundred children responded in unison, "I believe that I shall see the goodness of the LORD in the land of the living."

The words clanged against the arched ceiling, the echo covering us for what felt like an eternity. How was there so much sound? Had the stained glass, the stone Marys, the fourteen Jesuses all chimed in? Satisfied, the priest nodded, retreated to the rear of the church. Silence fell like a curtain, except for the pops and creaks of the pews under the shifting weight of the kindergarteners. Sister Sarto leaned forward, caught my eye. She didn't say a word, but her expression said it all: "Do your best to follow along, and remember, do not enter the Eucharist line."

For the uninitiated, Mass is a full-bodied, sensorial experience. There is a time to stand, a time to sit, and a time to kneel. There is both music and sacred silence. There are rote prayers even the youngest seem to know. There is a lingering sweet smell I couldn't name back then. And in my first Mass, I felt as though I'd entered a foreign country, one where I didn't know the language or customs. For almost an hour, my cheeks burned and my stomach churned. There was so much data to take in, but I couldn't make sense of it.

Before entering the sanctuary, Sister Sarto had warned me against entering the Eucharist line, which she explained was what I called "communion." Because I was not Catholic, I was not permitted at the Lord's Table, which I found a relief. If I could not enter the line, I would not trip on my shoelaces or step on the back of Jenna Kohler's Keds or find myself standing spotlight-frozen in front of the priest like an idiot in an art museum. Still, the good sister said, there'd be plenty of room for me at the passing of peace. So when Monsignor Galvin said, "Let us offer each other a sign of peace," Sister Sarto turned, extended her hand, and in her Irish brogue said, "Peace be with you."

And it was.

I was only ten years old, the new kid drowning in a sea of new religious conventions, but in that singular moment, when Christ's peace passed among the congregation of children and teachers, I felt something like an epiphany. Christ's peace—it is for all of us.

Some enter the Catholic Church as babies, pulled by history, family tradition, and the ancient sacrament of water. Others enter over long periods of time. They are pushed and pressed by some force heavier than the stone altar until they finally give in. I am in the latter category, and it'd take that first Mass and an additional three decades for me to give in to my ten-year-old epiphany at Immaculate Conception Church in Fort Smith, Arkansas. Why'd I give in? Because epiphanies don't let go of you, and neither do the places that give rise to them.

Childhood memories are full of fun house images—contours exaggerated or elongated or thickened. Still, these memories are mine, and they've stuck to my ribs like good bread for over three decades now. I have tried to shake them loose. It is impossible. Epiphanies might begin outside of us, but they root down, press in, haunt. Epiphanies and their mysteries—those painted and those passed in peace—began haunting me during the summer of Helga. They haunt me still. Both of those epiphanies were a product of place, space, and time.

Thirty years after the summer of Helga, Amber and I followed a Christian philanthropist and art collector as she walked us through her private collection. In an Orange County office building, we made our way through halls where art by accomplished artists hung. Tucked near the back of an archival room, a painting by a famed Christian artist was propped against a cabinet. The painting was layered with mineral pigments and gold leaf, the blue of my grand-mother's eyes, the blue of comfort.

As we toured the collection, the philanthropist decried modern church buildings as boring and "devoid of the sa-cred," by which she meant devoid of art, by which she meant devoid of catalysts for epiphany. She couldn't bring herself to worship in a renovated strip mall, a building with no architectural intrigue, no stone. What was beautiful about drywall and garish lighting arrays? Beauty in the modern sacred spaces, she said, is artificial, fading when the lights turn on. This was not the case in traditional sacred spaces, and then she shared something I can neither verify nor forget: when people stepped into the cathedrals of historical Christianity, they were stepping into an embassy of heaven. They were standing on holy, heavenly ground, and the architects and artists wanted to translate that reality in a storied way, a way the people could understand.

I'm no art historian, so I'm left to take her at her word. But imagine the audacity, the attempt to re-create heaven on earth. Also, imagine the sacred work of translating the awe of heaven to the common man. Imagine creating the conduits for epiphany.

I've heard some argue that the ornate cathedrals of Catholic and Anglican origins are antithetical to the teachings of Christ. Didn't he create space for the poor and outcast? Didn't he tell the rich young ruler to sell everything he had and give it to the poor? To be fair, their questions deserve to be asked. Should a church hold trillions of dollars of property filled with priceless art when billions of people live in poverty? And more to the point, are those spaces necessary to experience the love of Christ? After all, didn't Christ liberate his ministry from dedicated religious spaces? When Jesus met the woman at the well, didn't he refuse to declare the exact place she should worship? Didn't he tell her it was less about place and more about "spirit and truth"? And when Jesus found himself in despair, didn't he retreat to nature—the desert, the mountain, the garden—instead of the temple?

Just as I'm no art historian, I'm no theologian. But here's my hunch: there is a both-and in the conversation about sacred spaces. After all, Jesus spent time in the temple, a space dedicated to prayer and Scripture, and the temple of Jerusalem in Jesus's time was no drab space. There was plenty of gold and silver in that house of worship. But he also made his way to the desert, mountain, and garden.

There, away from the business of life, in the deep silence of ink-blue sky pinpricked by stars, Christ communed with the Divine Love. Both spaces held a certain kind of beauty. Both spaces were dedicated. Both spaces could be places of epiphany.

Human as we are, embodied as we are, we crave dedicated spaces, and our modern world proves this truth. We erect cubicles in corporate offices for dedicated workspace. We tier recliners in an oversized room with an oversized screen because we like to be comfortable when we watch the summer blockbuster. We train our bodies in gyms with treadmills or CrossFit boxes with kettlebells or yoga studios with blocks and mats. Social media platforms are marked by memes, opinions, avatars. Shouldn't we have dedicated spaces for silence, meditation, and prayer? Shouldn't we have embassies of heaven? Shouldn't those embassies convey the beauty of heaven, draw us to quiet contemplation of the place where the eternal glory of God dwells?

I was only a child when I visited the gallery, when I had my first real artistic epiphany. I was only a child when I attended my first Mass, but there was something about the beauty of that space that made sense to me too. Both spaces drew me in, both spoke to me, even as awkward as I felt. In that church, I longed for things of heaven, even if I couldn't have said it with so much clarity. And I still do.

Over three decades later, I stand in the presence of sacred art and recite prayers with my family and friends. We all go to the table together, and there I come into the epiphany of heaven. I'm part of an eternal family, one that will one day be perfectly reconciled to one another, perfectly reconciled to Christ, perfectly beautiful.

Still, there are other places, places outside of beautiful cathedrals or parish churches, that make space for epiphanies. Among those places is the White River.

Above the fog-skirted White River, a mountainside of fiery maples and oaks raise their arms over the tailwater pools. A new day washes down those deciduous embankments, down thousands of years of composted oak leaves and limestone mountain knees. The Ozarks welcome my son Isaac and me to the water, where rainbow trout rise for the morning meal. Every few minutes, one of those trout breaks the surface and leaps into the air for some small fly hovering above the water. Acrobat. Daredevil. Airborne hunter.

Thigh deep, Isaac lets his line out, then begins his rhythmic cast over the water. The rod bends, the tip pushing the line back and forth until his fly drops into a small eddy where the water turns back on itself. Fish are holding there, just on the other side, he says.

I am behind him, recording it all on my phone because his skill with the rod, the water, the hillside is a beautiful thing, and if I should ever lose my mind or memory, I want this moment to be memorialized. There, while recording, a scene from Marty Stouffer's *Wild America* plays out over Isaac's shoulder. Less than forty yards away, an American bald eagle leans forward on the crooked branch of a dead tree, pushes into the air, then dives toward the water. Legs extended, he reaches, and talons sharp as gaffer hooks pull up a trout that came too close to the surface. He flies out of frame just before Isaac's line tightens, and now he's fighting his own prey, his own trout struggling against line, rod, the muscles and tendons of a boy.

Isaac lands his trout, and I capture it on my phone before he releases it into the water. It darts back to its hiding place. We stand in awe of a singular moment, a moment in which all creation came together. It is a bone-deep awe that could never be conjured by a video game or any moment on any social media platform, one that could never occur in a bowling alley or movie theater. Here in our own personal liturgy, in the sacred silence of nature, I am reminded of the goodness of God in the land of the living. "This is my Father's world," I think, "I rest me in the thought of rocks and trees, of skies and seas—His hand the wonders wrought."[1]

There it is again in that dedicated sacred space, the spark of the sacramental. This is God's world, his place, and he is in, through, and over it all. In that epiphany, I find something like hope.

Amber: Under the Art of Monasteries

Seth and I recently took a trip to Italy with our dear friend Tsh and an amazing group of pilgrims. The people with us were from all different backgrounds, but it was our first time to visit as Catholics. We had also gone to Italy with Tsh before we had become Catholic, and that first visit was so full of heavenly tastes and smells that I knew I would be compelled to go back to Tuscany for the rest of my life. Nothing about that first trip made me want to be Catholic, though. Our introductions to the Italian church were led by tour guides who preferred to focus on the scandalous history of all the grossest popes—and there were quite a few of them. It was interesting, and it was appalling, and this was my takeaway from that trip: gelato, good; Catholic stuff, bad.

I would have called anyone a liar who had told me I'd be looking forward to a trip to Rome as a by-God pilgrim one day, but there we were, rosaries in our pockets, traveling on a tour bus to holy sites while watching videos on the in-bus video system about the saints (thanks, Bishop Barron!). One of our first stops was the Vatican. We visited the Necropolis—the catacombs—under St. Peter's Basilica, and though I knew where I was, I hadn't exactly wrapped my head around it. The day before, we had walked nearly twenty-eight thousand steps through Rome (yes, we got a little lost), and I'd already seen enough paintings and statues to provide many lifetimes of meditation prompts. Rome is a giant and always-awake city. Fountains spew water around the clock, and the air is thick with both historical and modern-day splendors and unrest. It's a lot to take in.

We stood levels beneath the altar in St. Peter's. Each level beneath the current altar is another altar built before it. One level is Constantine's "Old St. Peter's Basilica," built because of its proximity to Nero's circus, where Peter was said to have been crucified upside down. And because the Necropolis was just outside Nero's circus, the church long believed Peter was buried there. It only made sense. It was the burial site of both pagans and Christians—rich and poor alike. But was there any proof that Peter was buried here?

In her quiet accent, our guide explained how excavations of the site beneath St. Peter's Basilica, the place rumored to house the bones of Peter, began in the 1940s. There, under centuries of rubble, they discovered a wall covered in graffiti, and the words all over it were written to the apostle Peter. This graffiti wall was next to a low roof, and an altar was under it, built above a box that held bones wrapped in precious fabrics. Those bones are believed to be Peter's, in no small part because of the graffiti wall. According to one source, "In abbreviated form, St. Peter's name is present on the wall at least twenty times, usually accompanied by prayers for the dead person named—in one case expressing joy that the lost relative lay in the same cemetery that held Peter's own body."[2]

We had already learned on our first visit to Italy that you could be resting in a pew in a middle-of-nowhere town and look over to find a whole skeleton nonchalantly laid to the side. This is normal for Italians, and this might sound weird, but I like it. There is something about the bones of saints left behind. They lived as proof of Jesus in their own time, in their suffering, in their ecstasies, in their own flesh and bones, and Catholics believe they still exist in a metaphysical way among us as the great cloud of witnesses. So some churches keep the bones to remind us that beloved saints are in that great cloud. And of course, one day we may get to heaven, and all the members of that cloud may say, "Ew, gross. Why didn't you bury our corpses?" But so far as I understand it, those bones have drawn many deeper into the life of faith. They've served as tangible reminders that the person who owned the bones now sits in the unveiled presence of God. Somehow, those bones draw the pilgrims out of this world, up to the heavenly places in some quantum way. Faith makes many things so.

When our guide turned suddenly and quietly said, "If you would like to take a moment to pray here beside St. Peter, you may do so now," I stood there too long trying to process. She pointed in the direction of a cutout in the wall covered over with glass. There, behind that glass, we could see tiny fragments of . . . what? Bone?

Saint Peter? You who lopped off ears in protective bravado, who tried to walk on water, the passionate one I've always identified with the most—is it you? Does it matter? Look at the words that regular humans wrote on this wall. They all had different handwriting. People with different handwriting two thousand years ago called this place holy because they believed these bones to be yours.

The idea of Peter on the other side of that glass was too enormous. Then, as our crew started shuffling toward the exit and I saw the moment was about to pass, I crossed myself and said a prayer for my friend Annie in Nashville, who had begun a new journey in which she was asking God to make her more like Peter. Aside from my bewildered questions, that's all that came into my mind, but I was glad enough to think I might have written "St. Peter, pray for Annie" if I were the type to tag such a sacred place like the ancients were.

It was like this for me for a lot of the trip. My brain knew that what I was experiencing was amazing, but my heart was slow to feel it. I was quiet. I was supposed to be feeling waves of glory, and instead I was gathering data and filing it as quickly as possible so I could go back and read the files one day. That's not usually how I travel, but I couldn't sort out what was holding me back from experiencing all these things at an emotional level.

It was good to get on a bus and ride out of town the next day because my capacity for the city had been overly met. We needed a breather and gave our sweet tour guide a talking time limit because he could spend—and had spent—twelve hours in a single whack telling us every interesting detail of his country. Things finally went quiet. The fields opened up in different shades of blue, gray, and green, according to the way the cloud shadows fell. There were acres of drooping sunflowers in perfect rows. Long driveways led to homeplaces so old that you'd have imagined chariots, not modern Mercedes, out front. There were giant trees shaped like umbrellas, olive groves, and walls overhung with vining flowers I couldn't identify.

The drive took over an hour, and then the terrain became like home—similar to north Alabama and northwest Arkansas. We could tell we were climbing in altitude, and I opened an altimeter app on my phone to see how high we were above sea level, which is where we had been in Rome. We'd risen thirteen hundred feet, and below us was a beautiful valley. Soon after that, there was a sea of trees in every direction going down. Cell coverage disappeared, and we were officially remote.

We came to the place where we could drive no more, parked the bus, and got out. The older ones among us had the option to ride in a comically tiny car on the narrow path uphill toward our destination. The oldest among us was JuJu. She was seventy-nine years old, and when we had introduced ourselves at the beginning of the trip, when we had shared why we had come, JuJu said, "My dream all my life was to come to Italy. This will be my final trip." As we ascended the path straight up the mountain, we lagged behind JuJu most of the way. She had decided to walk. Just as I inhaled for a big *whew!* to echo through the trees, our guide (being funny) looked at us with serious eyes, pointed to her, and said, "I better not hear one of you complain." I swallowed it.

We became quieter, focusing on our breath. We were walking upward to Subiaco, which was built around the cave that is now called il Santo Speco, an important site of the Western monastic movement. St. Benedict of Norcia lived there as a hermit in the early sixth century, following the example of the desert fathers. Behind JuJu, we felt it. This journey to the cave is holy. She wanted to feel the climb, her labored breathing. She wanted to feel the cost of getting to the cave. She was on a pilgrimage to a sacred place, and we were following her, our real leader.

At the top, we entered a parapet courtyard, which, like the rest of the monastery, is built into the rockface of Mount Taleo. There we could hear no engine or horn. If it wasn't for the electric lights and flushable toilets in the visitors' bathroom, we might have thought we had stepped through a wormhole. An ancient air was about us, and the only sounds were cicadas, birds, bells, and our footsteps.

As we stepped through the rock doorway and into the monastery, the signs said *Silencio Perpetuo*, but we were told silence was no longer enforced. Still, no voices rang out, except I imagined they did in praise during Mass. I sensed I was in a place that kept the darkness out. I sensed myself opening, almost exposed. We stayed gentle, listening. Hydrangeas and roses had bloomed. Subiaco was a place to hear.

Inside is art from the eighth century and gorgeous architecture from the eleventh. A portrait of St. Francis there is said to be the oldest in existence. Francis took haven at Subiaco in 1223, and by the fourteenth century—just one hundred years after his refuge—vibrant frescos lined the inner walls and ceilings. As for those frescos, the characters on the walls had been painted in such a way—direction of the eye, light and shadow, emotional expression—that it seemed each was in conversation. It's astounding what you hear in silence.

When we walked into the nave of the upper church, it was like visual surround sound, a sort of synesthesia. I was neck-craning and jaw-dropping at the rich, deep, bright, and newly refurbished display of lapis lazuli, emerald green, scarlet, and gold. The eye doesn't know where to land without instruction, so I let mine go a bit out of order. I was first drawn to the ones I call "my ladies," the myrrh-bearing women, the ones with whom I'd like to keep an association, the ones whose likenesses hang in my own house. I noticed near them the story of Benedict as the great exorcist. He seemed to be giving a few whoopings in order to deliver a brother from a particularly nasty demon situation, because Benedict didn't keep room on that hillside for such things as demons.

Then I saw what should have first captivated me, what was straight ahead and wide across the wall: a scene of the crucifixion, Jesus on the cross with chaos spread out all below. The sky is rolling in black behind him, the kind of endless black that reflects no light. In the foreground is Mary, and there in the chaos, people are holding her back. Jesus's gaze is locked with hers, as if there wasn't another soul there. This is when I began to break, witnessing that mother love for a son, and the love of a son for his mother. What other thing do I know more than this? I cracked open, soft as petals, and tears started rolling down my face.

There were too many stories painted there to write about, but the one that haunts me still is the one that caught me last. On one side of Jesus are his disciples, the ones who'd witnessed firsthand his way of love, and between them stands Judas. Behind him are soldiers, and the painting is the very decisive moment of the kiss, when Judas signifies to the soldiers the one to be taken away. And what I saw in both Judas's and Jesus's eyes is pain. Jesus is heartbroken. He is all divine, must have known it was coming, but it didn't matter. It didn't save him from also being all human, someone who loved Judas. He knew every good thing about Judas, saw him playing in the olive groves as a child. He knew the friend, the inner child too. He knew his dreams and wounds. And quickly this is Jesus's goodbye. Nothing will be the same after this. Roosters will soon crow. Jesus will go the rest of the way—to be made naked, to be beaten, to be left alone to die.

Maybe it was the fresh empathy I'd found for one who'd lost his friend. I don't know, but a bomb went off inside me. Tears softened me when I saw the mother love in Mary as she hurt for and with her son. I had been moved by the women sticking their necks out to be with the one they loved, to follow through with their commitment to stick by his side. Then *BOOM!* I was shredded by deep betrayal, which I have felt in an ongoing way since I left Anglican ordination. The sense of betrayal followed me like a stench, and I hadn't been able to wash it off for three years. And out of nowhere, in that pain of betrayal, an even worse feeling overtook me.

I felt intense love for the one who had hurt me. I missed the part of him that was my friend, the good I know is in him because, even though he hurt me and others, I always also saw good. I had held out for that good. I sensed love in Jesus for him, the same love he holds out to all of us.

I looked up at the painting again, but this time Jesus was looking not at Judas but rather at me. That's when I knew it: every time I betray him, this same love is for me. Every time any one of us betrays him, this love is for us. There was darkness in me when I arrived at Subiaco, but in that moment, the darkness moved out. I may as well have been the one getting a Benedictine whooping.

Here is the miracle. When that darkness moved out, a body of light took over, and I became full. There was a throne inside me, though I hadn't known this. Love can be seated there, at my core, and love is not thwarted by betrayal. It is steady. It is clarifying. It exists no matter how deep the hurt, how serious the betrayal.

There, in that monastery, love was crowned within me. It didn't take away the ache of betrayal. It didn't negate the wrongdoing. It didn't tell me the pain would go away. It just showed me the actual feeling of forgiveness. I'd made the choice to forgive, but I hadn't felt it. When love took the seat, my losses could no longer be enthroned there. The pain remained, but it didn't reign. There just wasn't space for it there.

Space matters. Subiaco has mattered for centuries, but I couldn't stay there. I couldn't crawl into that cave like Benedict did, though I know how it feels to think that's a good idea. I had to return home, to my place among the people I love, some of whom are the ones who've hurt me the most, who've contributed to that feeling of betrayal.

I returned to our familiar sacred space and our rituals too. I sit in the pew behind Seth when he's leading worship in a whole new place, in the Mass at St. Joseph's. There I recite the Penitential Act. I examine myself and confess what I have done "through my fault, through my fault, through my most grievous fault." I ask who is on the throne, and I hear the story through the liturgy, again, fresh. Then, for those moments I allowed love to slip off the throne, I raise my voice with Seth and his coleader, Luke. With the entire congregation, I sing, *Kyrie Eleison, Christe Eleison*—Lord have mercy, Christ have mercy. There I can feel love taking the seat again, and it makes me cry bittersweet tears every time.

It's weird to feel freedom and for that freedom to hurt. It's not what I expected, but I don't know why I didn't expect it. Forgiveness didn't keep Jesus from being hurt. It didn't keep him from dying. But it did make a way for him to rise again.

Practice: Visit a Sacred Space

Maybe you don't have a sacred space you frequent. There's something powerful in calling a place sacred, all the more powerful when you aren't the only one calling it so. Aim to visit a sacred space on a regular basis. Does your local church have open hours when you can sit in silence and pray? Is there a room set aside for prayer and meditation? Consider visiting that space.

If you're not Catholic but you're feeling brave, consider checking the website of your local Catholic church to see if they have "adoration"—a time when you sit in the presence of the Eucharist. Adoration is open to everyone, and there you sit in the silence and meditate on the presence of Christ. Try it even if you think the Eucharist is all metaphor, even if you think it's not actually transubstantiated into body and blood. That said, if you choose to visit an adoration space, you might call ahead to see whether there's anything you need to know. For instance, I (Seth) sent my friend Shari Stewart to adoration at St. Martin of Tours Catholic Church in Louisville, Kentucky, and two whole skeletons were flanking the altar. That was certainly disconcerting, but it's also very rare.

Regardless of what you believe or what sacred space you choose for your own time of meditation and reflection, you'll find solace in that place. You'll find that when you give yourself to the beauty of a religious space, your heart can be drawn up toward epiphanies.

nine

FLIP THE SCRIPT

Seth: How Joy Subverts the War Machine

From the front, the rock house looked like that and nothing more. Its facade was a liar.

Built sometime in the early 1900s, it had burned in 1918 and was rebuilt around the charred Ozark stone bones the following year. There were additions in the 1930s, again in the 1960s. It was the Haines family homestead, a place owned by my dad's grandmother and grandfather before it passed to his folks. My mom lived in the attic while she finished her master's degree. Amber and I owned it for a brief spell in the 2010s before selling it because its ancient body—its plumbing, electrical conduit, and masonry—was beginning to break down, and young as we were, we simply didn't have the money to doctor the old lady.

We parted with that home, but the memories stick. Behind a door in the kitchen, a set of stairs led to an old stone basement filled with jars of jelly, tins of ancient kerosene, and ghosts. There was a useless fireplace right under the kitchen, and its chimney had long been sealed and plastered over. When I was a child, Grandma would send me down for a jar of preserves, and I would avoid laying eyes on that fireplace out of fear that some secret passageway would open, and a gang of zombies would come through and take me down into a dank Ozark cave.

Upstairs, a doorway led from the kitchen to the dining room and a shotgun living area so long they were separated by thin double doors. The side closest to the kitchen door was the combined dining area and formal living room, where we ate Kentucky Fried Chicken on Sundays before sitting to rehash my grandparents' trip to Hawaii in the early 1980s for the infinitieth time. On the other side of the double doors was the den, with a wall-sized stone fireplace and wood paneling so dark it soaked up all the light from the east-facing windows. In that cave, Grandpa took naps in his recliner while watching the Dallas Cowboys. There Grandma drank Dr. Pepper and read large-print editions of *Reader's Digest*.

The dining room, formal living room, and den were covered in thick, green carpet from the 1970s, which contained as much of Ms. Kitty's Siamese fur as it did carpet fiber. No vacuum on earth was strong enough to pull out all the shed from that one awful cat. All that dust and dander. Years of it. I was never in that house without an inhaler.

In the hall, stairs led to an attic, which had mostly been converted into a sort of bunkhouse and had that same shaggy carpet. One side of that bunkhouse had a small room with two beds and bookshelves filled with every volume of the Nancy Drew and Hardy Boys series. The other side had three beds, a bathroom, and a nook with a glass case. In that glass case were the effects of the dead.

As early as eight, I remember standing in front of that glass case, puffing on my inhaler and trying to make sense of the earth-colored skull on the left side. At some point, my grandpa had told me it was the head of a dead German, some man he'd killed in the war. Later, he confessed it was some skull they'd found on the property years ago. He never said it this way, but I suspect it was a sort of *memento mori* for him, a remembrance that life is a fleeting thing.

Beside that skull were reminders of his time in the war. There was a pitcher and cup set, brown and white speckled, with the emblem of his unit on the side—the Red Bull of the 34th Infantry. Beside that, a Red Bull patch, some Nazi money, a bayonet, and a framed German Mauser C96—a semiautomatic, which he said he had stripped from a Nazi soldier. Had my grandpa killed him? I'd never learn the answer to that question.

These things brought a gravity to the house, an anchoring to reality. There had been men who'd left family and friends, who'd traveled overseas to take up arms against the cloud of evil spreading across Europe. They fought for the boys laid to rest by Japanese bombs in Pearl Harbor. They fought for the French, whose city of love had been captured by hate. Even if they didn't know it at the time, they fought for the Jews, who were herded into camps as if cattle. My grandpa had seen it. He'd crawled through the despair of the Italian theater, killed men, lost friends, prayed that the great God who was Christ would bring him home to his family—my grandma, his boys, his church family.

My grandpa was on the outskirts of a small village in Italy when news of surrender reached him and the GIs. When they entered the village, he said, it smelled of fresh bread and perfume. Italian women came through unlocked and opened doors to meet them. Gone were the Nazis, the iron-jawed men of death riding war machines made in German factories. Gone was the black fog of fascism that had hung over the country. That night, the villagers feasted with the

American men—fresh bread and soup, maybe a little wine. That feast was a memorial meal. The Third Reich was gone. Italy, a country once asleep, had awakened.

The jug and mugs, the Red Bull patch, the pistol, the bayonet—I was drawn to these things because they spoke of the human struggle against evil. Also, they were implements of war—things that capture the imagination of boys—and they served as tangible reminders of the violence sometimes required to overcome antichrist evil. Other curios and figurines were scattered throughout the house that I paid less attention to. Small bird carvings, vases with dragons on them, old clocks, a candle carousel from some Scandinavian country. Among them were kitschy figurines of small, rosy-cheeked children. One held sheet music, lips parted as if singing. A little girl with a headscarf sat with a blackbird in her lap. One little boy held a basket, another an umbrella.

I didn't know much about those silly figurines except that they were old, German, and about as interesting to a boy as those cartoonish Precious Moments figures the old Baptist ladies collected. What I didn't understand then, and what I'm only beginning to understand now, is that those figurines—not the Precious Moments ones—were weapons in their own right. They were their own act of resistance against the Third Reich.

My parents were in attendance when our family was confirmed into the Catholic Church. Dad—a confirmed Catholic—gave each of my four boys a rosary made from Holy Land olive wood. My mother—a studied Presbyterian with no modicum of devotion to Mary—presented me with my confirmation gift, a white porcelain Madonna, and said, "I thought maybe she could keep watch over your kitchen."

The Madonna had been her great-aunt's, and my mother had received it from the estate. It had traveled all the way from Germany, where it was made. It was a Hummel.

The name Hummel meant very little to me, and she must have sensed that because she went on to describe other Hummel figurines I'd seen, figurines that were much different from my porcelain Lady. Traditional Hummels, she said, were smaller and were of children doing childish things, and this is when I knew exactly what she was talking about—those kitschy statues of children in Grandma's glass case. This one, though, was different. It was long and lean, and the teenage face of Mary tapered to a soft point. Her nose was not dainty but more like the nose of someone trapped between childhood and adulthood. Her hands were folded in silent meditation. There was no illusion of motion. She was a silent girl, preparing to bear the salvation for the whole world.

I placed Our Lady of the Kitchen on the shelf above the bowls, and that night, after my mother left, a question nagged at me: Why was this porcelain Mary so different from the cartoonish Hummel figurines? What was the draw to those figurines anyway? I had to know more, so I turned to the internet.

Berta Hummel was born on May 21, 1909. The third daughter of an established and successful Bavarian merchant, Adolf, and his wife, Victoria, Hummel did not know poverty. In fact, she didn't want for much. At five, she was enrolled in a school run by an order of teaching nuns. There she learned reading, writing, and art. At twelve, she was admitted to the Institute of English Sisters, where her artistic talent stood out. At the prodding of her father, she applied to the Academy of Applied Art in Munich and was admitted without being required to take the entrance exam. She excelled and at age eighteen graduated at the top of her class.

Now, if you know anything at all about world history, it's this: in the early 1930s, the Nazi Party was on the rise in Germany, and at its helm was Adolf Hitler. In a time of poverty coming out of World War I, he promised the people of Germany power and prosperity. Berta Hummel was interested in neither. She was more interested in simplicity and art, and so instead of trying to make a go of it as a commercial painter, she joined a Franciscan convent and adopted a new name. The artist formerly known as Berta had become Sister Maria Innocentia Hummel.

This is not to say that Sister Maria Innocentia Hummel gave up on art. She continued painting and sketching, but her work was sold to help support her sisters. And though she could have painted more sophisticated portraits, landscapes, or icons (she did on some occasions), she chose subject matter that stood in stark contrast to the darkness of the age— cartoonish children who often wore smiles, held hands, or examined a butterfly, frog, or angel with wide-eyed wonder.

Sister Hummel's art may have been simple and affected, but it was not weightless. In an age of nationalistic fervor, of a führer who continued to advance the myth of Aryan supremacy and the belief that a master race could assert global white supremacy, Hummel did what all great artists do. She painted in shades of subversion.

Sometime between 1933 and 1935, Sister Hummel created a charcoal and pastel work now known as *The Volunteers*. The piece depicts two children goose-stepping, one beating a drum while the other carries a rifle backward. Beneath it she'd inscribed *Lieb' Fatherland magst ruhig sein!* (Dear Fatherland, may you be at peace!). The subtext was not subtle: Dear Hitler, do not send our boys off to die.

Hummel's artwork did not go unnoticed. It grabbed the attention of the Nazi media machine, thereby grabbing the attention of Hitler himself. Hitler fancied himself an artist, and art historians agree he had some skill as a painter, even if his work was cool, aloof, and as detached from human emotion as the man himself. It was this detachment that led to his rejection by the Academy of Fine Arts in Vienna. When Hitler—a self-proclaimed artistic expert—saw Sister Maria's work, it burned him. This nun, who'd received an outstanding education in art, painted weak German children with "hydrocephalic heads" and club feet.[1] She should not be celebrated, he said. It was not art.

I found no indication that Sister Hummel responded directly to Hitler, but maybe her images contain a cryptic rebuttal of Nazi ideology. She often depicted children as angels, and in a time when Hitler was persecuting the Jews—men, women, and children alike—many of those angels had Stars of David on their tunics, and sometimes they were staring at Davidic stars in the sky. In 1936, she painted *Unser Aller Mutter* (Mother of Us All), a portrait of Mary on some African coast tending to two Black boys. Between 1938 and 1939, she drew three German boys at a crossroads, and on the crossroads, a sign with a single legible word: *Stop*. Was it a call to contemplation before choosing the path of war or the path of peace? Sister Hummel took her art—cartoonish images of joy—and she shoved it in Hitler's eye. She was punk rock before punk rock was a thing.

Her work captured the popular imagination, and throughout the 1930s, the porcelain manufacturer Franz Goebel collaborated with her to turn her drawings into figurines. Many of those figurines were eventually purchased and sent back to the States by American GIs. But after Hitler took notice of her, commercial reproductions of her works were banned in Nazi-occupied territories. Then in October 1940, the convent Sister Hummel called home was confiscated by the Nazis and turned into a sort of camp for their troops. Only 40 of the 250 sisters, including Sister Hummel, remained. There she continued to produce hundreds of works of art, though relatively few of them were sold commercially, and what the Nazis allowed to be sold—mostly to unsuspecting consumers in the United States—helped support the sisters. Of course, the Nazis skimmed a little off the top to help fund their war machine because evil always tries to co-opt beauty.

Though Sister Hummel would continue to sketch her joyous cartoons in an age of despair, she would not live to see full-scale production of figurines based on her images. The embargo on Hummel production was not lifted until 1946, the same year she succumbed to tuberculosis. On November 6, she joined the communion of the saints in heaven. She was thirty-seven years old.

With all that history, I examined Our Lady of the Kitchen more closely. On the back of the porcelain pedestal was her signature—M. I. Hummel. It was stamped onto that piece a decade or so after her death, but still, that was *her* signature, the way she might sign any of her artworks. It is an angular signature, one with many peaks and valleys, just like the course of her life.

I think about Sister Hummel a lot these days, in no small part because Our Lady of the Kitchen still watches over us. But I think about the other figurines my mom and sister inherited, some from Grandma Haines and some from other relatives: a blond-haired boy carrying pigs in a basket; another playing with rabbits, smiling; a little girl with windswept red hair holding flowers; another little girl feeding yellow chicks. Before I knew the history of Sister Hummel and these figurines, I would have said these were silly and unserious knickknacks. Now, I see them for what they are— little icons that, in the words of Dylan Thomas, "rage[d] against the dying of the light."[2]

This is, I think, the deep down thing about art. All art comes from the human capacity to create, a capacity gifted by the great Creator. And just as he looked into the darkness, into the void and said, "Let there be light," we're given the opportunity to do the same. We stare into the darkness around us, into our own abysses, and bring the light through acts of creation.

In no small part, that's exactly what this book has been about. It's Amber's and my attempt to stare into the darkness and say, "Yeah, it's dark . . . but look here . . . the light of hope still burns." In our journey, we discovered that we could tend to that light and keep it burning by participating with the sacramental, deep down things that demonstrate God's wild love for the world: nature, art, sacred spaces, bread, wine, the human extension of forgiveness. But tending to it meant something else for Amber and me. It meant bringing it to the page, translating it as a form of resistance against the darkness. It meant showing up with our God-given capacity for creation and sharing something of the beauty, truth, and goodness we've experienced, even in one of the darker seasons of our lives. It's that light that shines against the tyranny of the past. It's that light that leads us into hope.

Sometimes we don't have a say about whether the darkness rolls over us like a blitzkrieg, but we can still tend to the light of the deep down things, the light of hope. Keep that light burning. Let it move in and through your own acts of creation. Gift the light to others. Say to them in their darkness, "Rise, let us go from here" (John 14:31 ESV).

Amber: In Spite, Take Heart

Almost every one of our "vacations" in my youngest years was spent at my mamaw's house, down in the river bottomland of west Tennessee, three hours from our home in the Appalachian foothills of north Alabama. I was little enough to wonder why anybody would ever need to drive farther than that. I was also young enough to wonder why my aunt Cathy kept on having baby boys until there were four of them. (The joke keeps being on me, doesn't it?) Our family's special gift was baby making, I guess. I remember Daddy once saying that all it took for him and Mama to have another kid was eating supper together.

Mamaw had birthed five sons and a daughter, and I was one of eighteen grandchildren. This meant that when we went to Mamaw's, it was pure chaos, but the kind I loved. There were coffee pots percolating on the stove, dogs howling, some motor always growling in the distance. There was an eternal game of gin rummy going on at the kitchen table. As for us kids, somebody was always getting in trouble or hurt by being somewhere they weren't supposed to be. The fun of being in a mysterious rickety barn can only be outdone by the fun of using the rotten branches of a giant oak tree as balance beams. Even indoors, there was trouble to be had. In the side room, big cousins scared the little ones with terrifying stories like "Rawhide and Bloody Bones." You know, normal country kid stuff.

My deepest sleeps were in the next room over from the booming laughter of my uncle's bass-singing vocal cords. Every one of my aunts could sing the highest soprano, and once in a while, we pulled the songbooks out, and the chaos settled. These are the moments I remember most from my childhood visits to Tennessee.

Not one of us kids would have missed a minute of it. Not even a barn loft could keep us from piling onto the floor at their feet. My aunts, Josie and Teresa, carried us up high. The altos and tenors knew how to take the middle ground in varying ways. And then the bass reverberated through the floors, anchoring us to the Tennessee soil. We were all

Church of Christ, and so we had a full a cappella choir—no need or desire for instruments. There was a wood-burning stove in the middle of the room back then, hot to touch, bouncing back sounds that had to have belonged to heaven. We sang and made music from the inside out.

We were all pretty poor back then, and we all knew what it meant to go without. I know now that there was a fair amount of despair in the room, though the adults shielded us kids from it for as long as they could. But here's what I can tell you: even in the lack, when we were singing, there was great joy, and our songs of joy looked despair in the face and said, "Watch me."

I'm not a great soloist, but I can pick out and sing multiple harmonies for any song because I grew up immersed in such rich harmony, which is why I was a choir girl at school. Not only that, but I leveled up to show choir and could sing those harmonies in a god-awful chiffon dress while doing the grapevine and swinging around my partner. Show choir is the first thing that took me out of our three-hour travel bubble and widened my eyes a bit, and it trained me to read music well enough to earn a spot in all-state choir. That's where I had a gothic experience with music that I remember as nearly psychedelic.

Choir members from all over the state filled an auditorium at Auburn University. We were divided into two choirs, the freshmen with the sophomores and the juniors with the seniors. I was a young one, and when the choir of older kids began to sing Bach's "Come Sweet Death," by the second sentence, I no longer felt the seat beneath me. As the lyrics mentioned being led homeward, the parts split off, and each individual singer sang at the pace they wanted, over the top of each other, slow in parts or fast, all as soloists singing the same thing with their own timing. Overtones took the corners, and undertones rolled beneath us. We heard sounds like a sea of angels crying. The music twisted and married, pulled apart and echoed as if death had truly come, as if we'd found out we had been haunted all along. I thought my soul had lifted from my body. Each vocalist landed on a single note held long together, and then it was utter silence, not a dry eye in the room.

Because of that choral experience, I knew what King Saul felt like when David came to play his music to ease his terror (1 Sam. 16:14–23). A song about death—what could be more despairing to most humans who walk this earth—was subverted, turned into something jarringly beautiful. There was hope there, even though I couldn't have explained it in the moment.

Music can be a truth teller, and it can soothe us in spite of our aches, but there's bad music too. Dishonest music. Music that isn't subversive as much as it is dismissive, and we all know it when we hear it. There was a song we grew up singing in the Church of Christ. "Blue skies and rainbows, and sunbeams from heaven are what I can see, when my Lord is living in me." It was a sloppy wet day at summer camp when I first heard that song. I was near eight, and it was the stupidest song I'd heard in all my long life. I didn't have the language for it then, but I know what was in my heart: "It's raining, you ding-dongs." People who ignore the pain and don't see the rain—their music is not my music.

The Bible is full of my kind of music: David wrote songs about God ripping his enemies a new one, and several psalmists wondered if God had forgotten them, if they'd make it at all. A whole book of poetry describes all kinds of sex, and so, yes, this Book of Books is one for me. In the Scriptures, the people of God pour out poetry and song, even while surrounded by danger, betrayal, and calamity.

I especially love the story of Paul and Silas in the deepest cell of prison singing hymns to God with shackles on their feet (Acts 16:16–40). The other prisoners listened, probably confounded. How could they be singing? It was against every code, against despair, against the circumstance. Their hearts lifted, even the hearts of the worst among them. Sometimes a shift in the heart is mightier and more unexpected than a move between tectonic plates. But in this scene, both quaked. They sang, and the earth shook so hard the doors swung open and their shackles fell off. They were accused, then they were singing, and then they were free. There was some spite to their joy, some holy defiance that was more powerful than any addiction or set of chains. I believe this story, and I will stick to it as my greatest weapon. When despair strikes, I have learned from Paul and Silas that I can strike back in subversive, unexpected ways. I can show holy defiance in the face of despair, and one of the ways I can do that is through engaging tangible expressions of joy and hope. And I haven't learned this just from Paul and Silas. I've learned this from so many in the world around me.

One of my favorite ways to study holy defiance is online, following stories, videos, and images of #BlackJoy, #BlackBoyJoy, and #BlackGirlMagic. I can't stop paying attention to Tabitha Brown and her Afro named Donna, how she handles the rude glances with her genuine love for others because she carries the deep down knowledge that she is all-the-way beloved. Sometimes I'm simply and utterly blown away by the talent and beauty in the wide range of posts labeled with these hashtags, but it's way more than the beauty that moves me, and it's my job to see it. The authors of many of these posts admit to deep pain and deep lament because their lived experience and their present reality have been marred by a history of slavery and racism. But even in the face of that sorrow, they celebrate their belovedness, their image-bearing uniqueness, and their profound joy.

Sometimes the powers that perpetuate despair are monstrous, gnarly, and out in the open, like a white supremacy movement or spiritual abuse perpetrated by church leadership. Sometimes the powers come in a form of darkness caused by a long separation from someone we love. These realms of darkness are far too close for many to feel like they can find any joy or hope in the midst of them, much less by singing through them. I've been there, feeling as if I couldn't sing or do anything to participate with joy or hope, but I have also had the privilege of knowing good teachers along the way who showed me it must be done, teachers like Ginny Mooney.

Ginny is my feasting friend, and when we're together, we always get Turkish coffee and baklava. She has always been my feasting friend, and this was especially true when most of my days were being eaten up by grief over the loss of my vocation, over sorting out the ways I felt bamboozled by my former priest. We have an understanding between us. We don't talk around pain. We allow it to pull up a seat at the table like one in our innermost circle.

Ginny lost her beautiful first child, Eliot, ninety-nine days after he was born. The missing is palpable, so all the more, we get together and we feast. We look ahead to the supper table where we will be reunited with our babies and friends. We look forward to the table where there will be no remaining questions about spiritual abuse or racism or death or the loss of vocation or whatever. Our hope rests on this future table, and so, we bring that table to earth.

The trick is that feasting in hope, in holy defiance of despair, doesn't count if you're always feasting. It's not defiant feasting if your children are perfect, if you aren't a huge disappointment to others, if you haven't been betrayed, or if your marriage requires zero work. It only counts if you know heartache, loss, or years of fruitless labor. It's in light of the deepest ache that we click the cup and feast and look forward to the great feast table and say, "Darkness, you haven't won."

But how do you do it?

Start by recognizing pain. Say, "Sure, maybe I'm the mustard in the middle of a crap sandwich," because it might be true. The world out there is unusually unfair. But here, between us with our living hope, our gray hairs are beautiful, and we feel an unexpected kindness so rich that we can't help but make another date to celebrate it all again soon. Agree with your feasting companions to eat big in hope of the great big future feast. Then eat the fat. Lick the plate. Always get the baklava. This way of feasting in hope rids our feast of any trace of gluttony because we're not eating fine food just to eat fine food; we're eating as if to say, "Even in the dark times, God gives us very good things."

John Ray, another of our dearest friends, stood at the front of the crowd on an unexpectedly warm October evening just before sunset. Papa John is one of the giants in my eyes, a man with a Texan hat, vintage Austin funk, a voice like Johnny Cash's, a smile as kind as Jesus's, and he's suffered the unimaginable. He lost his daughter Olivia to an inebriated driver who ran through a crosswalk, and when you are with John or any of the other Rays, Olivia is always just behind the veil. She is very close, and she was close that evening in October.

John was holding it together just fine at the front of us all, but then his two oldest grown daughters, Hope and Hannah, came around the corner with flowers. Neither of them was the bride, but they were visions, because their full story, their full beauty walked down the aisle with them. Olivia was with them, just as she was with John. We all felt it brimming in our eyes. Then our Naomi—who some might lovingly describe as a bull in a china shop but who I say is rather like a mosaic over and against a world full of so much bull—came out on her mama's sequined arm, and Jane walked her girl down the aisle. They stopped right in front of John, the presiding minister at Naomi and Zane's wedding, and all I could think, as one of many there in the middle of a full-on ugly cry, is that it felt like a birth. Like anguish and some of the purest joy I'd ever witnessed.

There's something about people who have suffered together. They know how to throw down. They know how to claim their joy when it's theirs to have. After the wedding, after a barbeque feast and tequila cocktails, we danced like we were saving the world. I think that in some small way, we were, because even in the grief of missing a sister, Naomi and all the Rays threw a party that testified: there is darkness, but this is not a dark place.

Earlier that evening, I had stood alongside another friend who's processing some destruction that has affected his vocation, his community, and his family. I imagine what he's going through feels like it's permeated everything. We stood there, and he pointed over to our friend Mike Rusch. Mike has asked him over and over again to hang out, he said. He didn't want to do it at first, but after feeling forced by Mike's bulldog persistence, he realized that being with Mike was the very thing keeping him attached to reality. Through presence—eating, drinking, exercising—Mike had brought him some of the only moments of hope and joy he'd experienced over the last several months.

That night, my weary friend said, "You know that verse where Jesus says, 'In this world you will have trouble, but take heart, I have overcome the world'?"

165

"Of course," I said.

"None of this pain is a surprise," he said, "and it's probably not going away. So, Amber, we may as well take heart." Whoosh. The words "take heart," especially in light of his deep pain, were like some holy middle fingers in the face of injustice. Jesus has overcome the world, and my friend was experiencing that through the presence of another friend.

Let me tell you what will mess somebody up in the best of ways, what will level the playing field when grief and despair come calling, what will bring justice and mercy and heap the hottest, kindest coals: hope and joy. Hope and joy flip the script when they sit with a friend who's lost their vocation. Hope and joy flip the script when they dance in the midst of loss. Hope and joy flip the script when they choose the friend going through the darkest day. In the midst of despair, hope and joy help us and others "take heart."

I wish I could say the Catholic Church was known for its singing in the way my church was growing up, but, Lord help us, it's not. Many of the songs we sing are from the Catholic charismatic renewal days of the 1960s and 1970s, which sounds like a thing my woo-woo heart would love, but they tend to be terrible. There's an old hymn, though, that I sang many times before I really heard it: "How Can I Keep from Singing?"

> What though the tempest around me roar,
> I hear the truth, it liveth.
> What though the darkness around me close,
> Songs in the night it giveth. . . .
>
> When tyrants tremble, sick with fear,
> And hear their knells ringing;

When friends rejoice both far and near,
How can I keep from singing?

No storm can shake my inmost calm,
While to that rock I'm clinging.
Since Love is Lord of heaven and earth,
How can I keep from singing?[3]

The backdrop of hope in this song is rage, the tempest, darkness, the river of grief, and the abuse of a tyrant. There is no good singing—no hope or joy—without being honest about the pain, loss, betrayal, or injustice and feeling some holy spite toward it. Hope and joy take a swing at all the tyrants, abusers, and thieves. Like love, hope is a verb, a thing that can be done.

We know hope and joy when we see them embodied and acted out, particularly by others who've gone through their own seasons of despair. We know hope and joy when they hold us and feed us when we're hungry. We know them on dark days even when we are all alone, when we choose to get out of bed to eat something. We know them when we make the decision to get up and brush our teeth even when we don't feel like it because we hope there will be a day when we want to smile again. We especially feel them when we feast and dance and drink the wine with dear friends even when pain is in the room with us.

And when we come through our own despair, when we've pushed through in hope and found joy, we carry that hope to others. We show up time and again for a friend or a child who struggles with despair. We convey hope when we hear a friend's story, when we say, "I believe you. Now tell me, what do you need?" We show hope when we're willing to go to our grave believing in good for those mired in despair, even though there are no signs of relief. We show hope when we verb it out to others in spite of the pain.

My beautiful garden with peonies, irises, astilbe, dahlias, veronica, false indigo, and every perennial herb I knew to plant—it all sold to some of our dear friends, Chris and Shelby. I was sad to leave that house, the boulders, the garden, but it was time. Selling our house was the end of an era, saying goodbye to the place of my healing, the first COVID years, and the beginning days of when Jesus became our balm through the Catholic Church. It was a balm, too, to know I was passing my work along to friends who wanted to learn to care for the soil.

We had to sell so we could build a home on our land in Goshen. In my grief over leaving behind my garden, I drove to Goshen regularly and walked through neck-high grasses to the place of my future rows of tomatoes, okra, and sweet corn. Even before we had a construction loan to build the house, I knew I couldn't go through with building a house without a plan for where the new dahlias would grow. Where will the asparagus be? The roses?

I imagined mornings with a screened back porch, black coffee, muck boots. This is where my walkway will be, and then here will be my gate. I counted my steps in a giant rectangle and figured out how big the garden would be, just far enough between the two trees that drop walnuts on either side. Even before all this planning, almost as soon as we bought the property, I planted blackberries, and they've grown and seem healthy in spite of intense drought and heat. I called a fence company and asked for an eight-foot-tall fence to protect it all from the deer. If I've learned anything, it's that the deer will come.

I walk around my fence now and go in and out through the gates. I wonder how I'll pull any of it off. I sit in a fold-out chair facing the field behind ours. It belongs to my farmer friends who don't intend to sell land in their lifetime. They intend, instead, to be our neighbors, to rotate cattle and sheep, and to wave at us along the way.

The johnsongrass is tipped with feathery seed heads, and the wind moves through them like a hand, in waves. The hills are the backdrop, and the sun sets just beyond them, right over where we host the farmers market. I will beat into the soil here and find enough rocks to build a mountain. I will feed the earth and let it feed me. I will pick blackberries and re-create Mrs. Mary's jam. This is my imagination at work, a joy so great that it is worth the move.

This is what I know now: the tempest and tyrants are real. They came into my life without invitation. Those tempests and tyrants still rear their heads from time to time, whether in my memory or in a social media post by those who've refused to acknowledge my pain. But here's what else I know, and I know it best from being a mother: despair is driven out by the hope of joy.

When in labor, when all is water, blood, and shit, and life or death hangs in the air as if on iron hooks, when the voice goes gravel and animal, and skin rips open, a mother pushes, and the hope of joy makes labor possible.

When labor passes, when meeting a child face-to-face for the first time, when the hope of joy is personified in your own flesh and blood, you know you wouldn't trade that suffering for anything.

I can say this now without equivocation: I know what it means to push through despair in the hope of joy. I know what it means to sing songs in the sadness. Yes, my kids are a reminder. Yes, the table, the feast, is a reminder. Yes, unashamedly shaking my rear end all the way to the ground while dancing at a wedding is a good reminder. But there is a better reminder. In the evenings, I take my washcloth, wipe away the makeup from the day. I stand there, looking into my own eyes, and though I'm no longer a curate, though I'm no longer on a path toward ordination, though I'm no longer anything other than Mary Amber Haines, wife and mother, I recognize myself. And there, Christ, the Divine Love, recognizes me too.

How can I keep myself from singing?

Practice: Hold a Feast

The world will do what the world does. It will come with pain, with anxiety. It will threaten to hold you under the river of grief. But if we are people of the Divine Love, if we have an unfading hope, there is good news. Even in the grief, even in the pain, we can feast as a form of resistance.

Gather people close to you, people who know the dark moments of your own life. Set a table. Create a spread. Ask those people to bring a dish, a piece of poetry, some art, something they've created or some creative thing that speaks to them. As you eat the fat and lick the plate, share that creative thing and ask what it evokes. Tell some jokes too. Laugh. Maybe sing a song. Feast one month. Then feast the next. And the next. As you do, remember: you and your people are a force of resistance against despair.

ACKNOWLEDGMENTS

It's strange that Joseph and Lindsey Mason don't come up very much in this book, because they have been companions through every part of this story. These are the friends who stood firm and spoke the truth with clarity in the midst of blinding chaos. They stood with us even at the risk of their own loss, and as we stepped into our despair, they came with us. They risked stepping into the darkness with no promises for how any of us would get out of it. As we write this, our friendship is nearly eighteen years old. It's an adult now, and it's threadbare in places but also proud, protective, tough, practiced, and very gentle. Above all, our friendship is an icon of hope. As the four of us began to realize that we had lost our home church together, we were also realizing that we had found home in the Catholic Church—apart from them. It was another layer of devastation and yet we stuck together every way we could.

Years ago, we took a family vacation with them in Colorado, which is where they'd chosen to move to live like paupers with their four kids so they could both attend seminary. One night, the four of us slipped away to eat at a French restaurant in Breckenridge, and Joseph—a third-culture kid raised in France—ordered all our food and wine without using a lick of English. It was a tiny place, and our waiter was gregarious and generous, bringing dish after dish for us to try. One other couple was in the room. After a while, they invited us to their table, and we all clinked our glasses together and began telling stories. The man was a wealthy banker named Angel. He was powerful and sweet, asked good questions, and poured exquisite wine. Hours went by. I have freeze-frames of it all in my mind. The corks across the table. The hospitality that passed between us. Nothing was withheld. We rubbed our faces from such immovable smiles.

At the end of the late night, as the room was shutting down, Joseph grabbed the check for the six of us over the objections of the well-to-do businessman. We got in the Masons' minivan to drive away, and we roared with laughter all the way home. Joseph was the poorest man I knew. The banker might have been the wealthiest man I'd ever met. How long did it take Joseph to pay off the wine tab? Who knows, but it didn't matter to him. He has always been like the real Jesus to us—serving the rich and poor alike—and Lindsey is no different. Over those dark months when I trudged along in my despair, what a light this scene was to me. Thank you, Joseph and Lindsey, for being with us through so many of life's feasts and famines. You are the very best of friends.

There were others who struggled alongside us during the darker season. We wouldn't have made it without the friendship of Nicholas and Angela Sammer and Jesse and Ashlyn Gagnon. We know it wasn't easy. We love you and we're so grateful.

We couldn't have done any of this without the support of our Brazos team, especially our genius editor, Katelyn Beaty. Thank you for taking a chance on this story.

We thank each of our siblings and our parents for encouragement as we wrote, especially SuSu and Daddy-O (Susan and Ron Haines), who opened their home so we could write away from kids and who kept an endless drip of coffee going.

We're grateful to our four boys and the friends they've brought along with them. You make it all worth it. We love you and we like you and we think about you every day and every night. We really do. You are each a light to us, even on your messiest days. Thanks for loving us on ours too.

Amber would like to thank a few others on her home team: Lindi Phillips, Becky Carter, Ginny Mooney, Brett Dickhut, Liz Mashie, Emily Jost, Brian Hirschy, Stephanie Mass, and always the Ray family—for your encouragement and presence. I never lost the feeling of home or hospitality in any of you.

To my "Somewheres," what a powerful voice we are together. We never shy away from the real story. You never stop expecting me to march even toward terrifying things so I can be healthy and help others find health too. Thank you.

There's also the good gift of friendship across the miles in this strange and lonely world as a writer. Laura Tremaine, Sarah Bessey, Nish Weiseth, Shannan Martin, Emily Freeman, Annie Downs, Sara Billups, Lore Ferguson, and Jessica Herberger, your voices, opinions, pushback, prayers, and lit candles have mattered to me in profound ways through several stages of this journey. Thank you.

Aside from those already mentioned, Seth would like to thank the group of scoundrels who are out of shits to give: John Blase, Winn Collier, and Kenneth Tanner. To the other Kindred (you know who you are): you keep me writing when I'd rather put down the pen, and this is no small thing. To the Substack community who funds my writing—creatively, monetarily, spiritually—thank you for living *The Examined Life* with me.

We're especially grateful for the group of early readers who gave us honest feedback, including Bob and Shari

Stewart and Stephen Carter. The weight of words is much to carry, and you've done it well over the years.

To those who've almost given up: We acknowledge you and your pain. Don't give in to the shadows. There is a banquet table in the valley where the cups overflow. Keep going.

NOTES

Chapter 1 Know the Hope of Saints

1. Gerard Manley Hopkins, "God's Grandeur," in *Gerard Manley Hopkins: Poems and Prose* (New York: Penguin, 1985), available at https://www.poetryfoundation.org/poems/44395/gods-grandeur.

2. Dana Gioia, foreword to Gerard Manley Hopkins, *The Gospel in Gerard Manley Hopkins: Selections from His Poems, Letters, Journals, and Spiritual Writings*, ed. Margaret R. Ellsberg (Walden, NY: Plough, 2017), 81.

3. Hopkins, "God's Grandeur."

4. Ellsberg, in Hopkins, *Gospel in Gerard Manley Hopkins*, 156.

5. Gerard Manley Hopkins, "As Kingfishers Catch Fire," in *Gerard Manley Hopkins: Poems and Prose* (New York: Penguin, 1985), available at https://www.poetryfoundation.org/poems/44389/as-kingfishers-catch-fire.

6. C. S. Lewis, "The Inner Ring," C. S. Lewis Society of California, https://www.lewissociety.org/innerring.

7. Joseph Pearce, "Standing on the Shoulders of Giants," *Faith & Culture*, February 21, 2019, www.faithandculture.com/home/2019/2/12/standing-on-the-shoulders-of-giants.

Chapter 2 Tell the Story

1. E. E. Cummings, "I Thank You God," Harvard Square Library, accessed January 19, 2023, https://www.harvardsquarelibrary.org/poetry-prayers-visual-arts/e-e-cummings-i-thank-you-god.

2. St. Ignatius of Loyola, *The Autobiography of St. Ignatius: The Account of His Life as Dictated to Father Gonzalez by St. Ignatius*, ed.

J. F. X. O'Conor (New York: Benziger Brothers, 1900), 19, available at Project Gutenberg, https://www.gutenberg.org/files/24534/24534-h/24534-h.htm.

3. St. Ignatius, *The Spiritual Exercises*, first annotation, trans. Louis J. Puhl (Chicago: Newman Press, 1951), available at https://spex.ignatian spirituality.com/PuhlTranslation.html4.

4. St. Ignatius, *Spiritual Exercises*, sec. 214 ("Rules with Regard to Eating: Fifth Rule").

Chapter 3 Find God in the Stuff of Earth

1. Henry David Thoreau, *Walden*, chap. 5.

2. Cited in "Cardoner Vision," Ignatian Spirituality, accessed March 1, 2023, https://www.ignatianspirituality.com/cardoner-vision.

3. St. Ignatius, *The Spiritual Exercises*, sec. 230 ("Contemplation to Attain the Love of God"), trans. Louis J. Puhl (Chicago: Newman Press, 1951), available at https://spex.ignatianspirituality.com/PuhlTranslation.html.

4. Flannery O'Connor, letter to Elizabeth Hester, December 16, 1955, cited in J. F. Desmond, "Flannery O'Connor and the Symbol," *Logos: A Journal of Catholic Thought and Culture* 5, no. 2 (Spring 2002), https://muse.jhu.edu/article/20417/summary.

Chapter 4 Create Signs

1. Norman Maclean, *A River Runs Through It and Other Stories* (Chicago: University of Chicago Press, 1976), 118.

2. J. R. R. Tolkien, *The Fellowship of the Ring: Being the First Part of the Lord of the Rings* (New York: Ballantine Books, 1954), 193.

3. Tiernan Ray, "AI Still Writes Lousy Poetry," ZDNET, June 3, 2021, https://www.zdnet.com/article/ai-still-writes-lousy-poetry.

Chapter 5 Practice Silence

1. Seth Haines, *The Book of Waking Up: Experiencing the Divine Love That Reorders a Life* (Grand Rapids: Zondervan, 2020), 201.

2. Robert Sarah, with Nicolas Diat, *The Power of Silence: Against the Dictatorship of Noise* (San Francisco: Ignatius, 2017), 71–72.

3. Erling Kagge, *Silence: In the Age of Noise*, trans. Becky L. Crook (New York: Pantheon, 2018), 83, quoting Fridtjof Nansen.

Chapter 6 Name the Knots

1. "Can't You See," featuring The Notorious B.I.G., track 8 on *Total*, Bad Boy Records and Arista Records, 1996.

2. Daniel A. Cox, "Men's Social Circles Are Shrinking," Survey Center on American Life, June 29, 2021, https://www.americansurveycenter.org/why-mens-social-circles-are-shrinking.

3. David Brooks, "The Crisis of Men and Boys," *New York Times,* September 29. 2022, https://www.nytimes.com/2022/09/29/opinion/crisis-men-masculinity.html.

4. Bethany Ao and Aubrey Whelan, "Impact of Covid-19 Shutdown—and Now Police Brutality—May Cause Increase in 'Deaths of Despair,'" *Philadelphia Inquirer*, June 5, 2020, https://www.inquirer.com/health/coronavirus/coronavirus-covid-19-deaths-of-despair-anxiety-depression-unemployment-20200601.html.

5. "AACAP Policy Statement on Increased Suicide among Black Youth in the U.S.," American Academy of Child & Adolescent Psychiatry, March 2022, https://www.aacap.org/aacap/Policy_Statements/2022/AACAP_Policy_Statement_Increased_Suicide_Among_Black_Youth_US.aspx.

Chapter 7 Make Amends

1. Buddy Wakefield, "Hurling Crowbirds at Mockingbars," available at "Buddy Wakefield: Elephant Engine High Dive Revival," YouTube video, 5:58, posted by speakeasynyc on December 27, 2009, https://youtu.be/bHX3qtJlmdU.

2. "Making Amends in Addiction Recovery," Hazelden Betty Ford Foundation, August 4, 2020, https://www.hazeldenbettyford.org/articles/making-amends-addiction-recovery (emphasis added).

3. Hazelden Betty Ford Foundation, "Making Amends in Addiction Recovery."

Chapter 8 Search for Epiphanies

1. Maltbie D. Babcock, "This Is My Father's World" (1901).

2. "Necropolis (Scavi), Graffiti Wall G, The Bones of St. Peter," St. Peter's Basilica, accessed January 19, 2023, http://www.stpetersbasilica.info/Necropolis/Wall%20G.htm.

Chapter 9 Flip the Script

1. Scott Simmons, "Meet the German Nun Whose Art Irked the Nazis," *Fort Meyers Florida Weekly*, May 25, 2022, https://fortmyers.floridaweekly.com/articles/meet-the-german-nun-whose-art-irked-the-nazis.

2. Dylan Thomas, "Do Not Go Gentle into That Good Night," in *The Poems of Dylan Thomas* (New York: New Directions, 1971), 239, available at https://poets.org/poem/do-not-go-gentle-good-night.

3. Robert Lowry, "How Can I Keep from Singing?" (1868).

Amber C. Haines is the author of *Wild in the Hollow: On Chasing Desire and Finding the Broken Way Home* and *The Mother Letters*. **Seth Haines** is the author of *Coming Clean: A Story of Faith* (winner of a *Christianity Today* Book Award of Merit) and *The Book of Waking Up: Experiencing the Divine Love That Reorders Life*. Together with Tsh Oxenreider, he cohosts the podcast *A Drink with a Friend*. Amber and Seth have experience speaking at conferences and events. They live in Fayetteville, Arkansas, with their four boys.

www.ingramcontent.com/pod-product-compliance
Lightning Source LLC
Chambersburg PA
CBHW020354100426
42812CB00001B/58